A SNEAKER ON MY PILLOW

Lessons for business. Lessons for life.

by Ralph Yourie

Published by:

FriesenPress

Suite 300 – 852 Fort Street

Victoria, BC, Canada V8W 1H8

www.friesenpress.com

Distributed to the trade by The Ingram Book Company

Table of Contents

A FEW ACKNOWLEDGEMENTS...

Four people are responsible for the writing of this book...the least important of whom is me.

For nearly thirty years, my wife Diane has believed in me far more than I could ever believe in myself. She deserves a great deal of credit for just about everything that I have accomplished over the past three decades.

The other two, each of whom I must acknowledge and thank, are Jeff Rein and Laurie Meyer. Since 1985, I have made my living as a manager with Walgreens, the nation's largest retail drug store chain. Writing is simply my favorite hobby. Several years ago, I began writing a weekly column for the benefit of my employees and colleagues. Some articles were business related. Others were life lessons. I enjoyed writing the pieces, and they were generally well received.

In 2007, Laurie Meyer was Walgreens' head of corporate communications. A few of my articles fell into her hands, and she rather enthusiastically passed them along to Jeff Rein, who was President and CEO at the time. Jeff also liked what he saw, which in turn led to my reaching a much greater audience. Jeff and Laurie have since retired, but we have remained in touch via email. I value them both as mentors and friends.

Not too long ago, I received a phone call from Jeff asking if I had copies of all that I had written. I did. He believed that there was a definite market for my work, and urged me to consider publishing it. That is how this book came into being. "A Sneaker On My Pillow" is the title of one of my favorite pieces.

I consider myself a rather modest person. While I know I write well, I am acutely aware that there is always a large chasm between what is good and what is good enough. Thank you Diane, Laurie and Jeff for believing in me. This book is a direct reflection of your encouragement, enthusiasm, and unwavering support.

A SNEAKER ON MY PILLOW

I am very close to my sister Mary. She is two years older than me, and currently lives in South Florida. We routinely vacation together, sharing a house for a week or more, enjoying each other's company. We have also been known to call on short notice and say "Life is getting too crazy here. Do you think you could put up with me for a few days?" Naturally, the door is always open.

Like most siblings, we had our share of battles growing up. While I don't recall what the fight was about, I do recall one time when we had a particularly harsh and bitter disagreement. It was probably over something silly like whose turn it was to dry the dishes, or who used something belonging to the other person without first asking. Stupid stuff, but I was nine and she was eleven. Kids that age are prone to getting riled up about such matters. The argument occurred in the morning and we didn't speak to each other for the entire day.

Later that night, a particularly violent thunderstorm passed through. There was heavy rain, high winds, thunder and lightning. Lots of lightning. It's just folklore, but we had often heard that since rubber doesn't conduct electricity very well, if you wore sneakers or rubber-soled shoes you wouldn't get hit by lightning. This isn't true, but we believed it. That night I went to bed still angry and still very much afraid of the storm. When morning came, the storm had passed, and I awoke to find Mary's sneaker resting on my pillow.

Navy sailors can be a tough, hard-headed, scrappy group of guys. When you are out to sea for an extended period of time, tensions will often run high. The hours are long and the work can be dirty and dangerous. It isn't long before patience runs short and tempers flare. While it was never condoned, it was generally accepted that every once in a while, fists would fly.

On a hot night in January 1979, my ship, the USS Shenandoah was tied to the pier in Guantanamo Bay, Cuba. A group of us were relaxing at the Enlisted Club on base when a fight broke out between Steve and Ray, two very large, very brawny, and very drunk boiler technicians. It is safe to say that the fight was about something stupid. Ray gave Steve a black eye, and Steve rewarded Ray with a bloody lip. Two days later, the ship was conducting a training exercise offshore when disaster struck.

A fire broke out in the engine room, filling the chamber with thick black smoke. Ray was working the boilers. Steve was on the firefighting team. Steve was among the first members of that rescue squad to arrive on the scene. Ray was the first life that Steve saved that day, carrying him up a metal ladder and away to safety.

As managers we are sometimes called upon to mediate disputes between employees who just can't seem to get along. It is one of those tasks that I really dislike doing, because if we all acted like adults it wouldn't have to be done. Personally, I wish that the parties involved would just beat each other up for a while, then shake hands and walk away as friends. Isn't that what really happened between myself and Mary? Didn't that also happen with Steve and Ray?

Most disputes are over something petty - like who works harder, or who is getting away with doing something that they shouldn't be. Once in a while, it is a personal issue that is not directly related to work. In most cases, it's simply two personalities that just don't mesh very well. Both employees may be hardworking, valuable assets to the company, but their constant bickering hurts both morale and productivity. In each of these cases I can't help but wonder - If the other person was in danger, would there be a sneaker on his or her pillow? Would there be a helping hand to pull him or her away from the fire?

A family is only as strong as its love, and the willingness of its members to support and protect each other. If a military unit does not work together in relative harmony, battles and lives will be lost. A business must also operate as a team, with each member respecting and supporting each other. This is required if the company is to grow and prosper. This does not mean that individuals must always care for, love or even like each other. Rather, it requires putting those differences aside for the good of all concerned. It means offering a sneaker or a hand to anyone in need when the rest of the team is counting on it.

A CAPTAIN AMONG CAPTAINS

Unless you are over a certain age or a big fan of sports movies, the name Mike Eruzione probably doesn't mean much to you. Mike was the captain of the 1980 U.S. Olympic hockey team. This was a team of amateurs that beat professional teams from Russia and Finland to win the gold medal, while playing against some incredible odds. Like many people my age, I remember sitting on the sofa with family and friends as we watched those two games with tears streaming from our eyes. If you are not familiar with the story, find a copy of the movie Miracle, and you will understand.

Often it comes down to leadership. My definition of the term is "the quality of an individual that enables him or her to represent and guide others successfully." Mike Eruzione was the dominant leader of that team, but not the only one. Mike has been quick to point out that while as captain he had to play a key role in holding things together and moving the group forward, he was only one leader among many. He played on a team that was filled with talented people, many of whom at one time or another had served as captains of other organizations. Mike was a captain among captains.

This example is certainly true in business as well. In fact, it is a common occurrence in almost any group or organization. There is a designated leader, but many others will share in leadership roles. Talented people are naturally inclined to step up and take charge when the situation warrants it. Some may have previously served in management roles. If handled properly, it can take a tremendous burden off any captain to know that others are willing and capable to share in leadership responsibilities.

What does it take to be an effective leader? I assure you that the title of "captain" or "manager" or "executive" has nothing to do with it. Eruzione understood this point. Leadership means you lead by example, holding yourself to a higher standard than others. It means that you don't panic when things get tough and you don't gloat when things go well. You share the praise and accept the blame. You learn what motivates your teammates and you use that knowledge effectively. You know when to step in, when to step up, and when to step aside. Most of all, through your actions, you earn the respect of others at all levels. People don't have to like you. It makes it easier if they do, but it isn't necessary. What is necessary is that they respect you, trust you, and want to follow your lead. You cannot learn leadership from a book.

I have been a captain for a very long time, in various positions and venues. At every level, I have found it vital to share the role. I have always been a captain among captains. If you are a successful leader, then chances are you already understand this. If you are a role player who is capable of rising to an occasion, then please do so. Use your leadership to help the organization succeed. You may not have the title, but if you are a true leader, you do not need it.

If my definition of leadership is correct, then Mike Eruzione was indeed a great leader. He proudly and successfully represented and guided that hockey team. He assumed the burdens, but shared them with others on his team. Those qualities led him and his team to Olympic gold. Those qualities made him a captain among captains.

A DOG STORY

One of our family dogs is a twelve-year old beagle named Truman. We got him as a puppy for my daughter Allison when she was seven years old. He was named Truman after the U.S. President because like Harry S. Truman he is strong, decisive, stubborn, and a bit of a politician. We also wanted to make sure we had named him before bringing him home; otherwise the poor dog might have wound up with a name like Spot or Cuddles.

Truman is having a rough year. The average life expectancy of a beagle is twelve years, so we had to expect him to start having health problems. Truman's primary health concern is a condition called Cushing's Disease. It affects the adrenal glands, which in turn affect a lot of other bodily functions. One of the more serious symptoms of the disease involves the deteriorating of joints, specifically the hips and knees. Joint problems, along with a weakening of his hind leg muscles had caused Truman to walk with an unsteady limp.

Recently, Truman's misfortune took a sudden turn for the worse. My family was sitting at home one night, watching television, when I suggested that a dish of ice cream would be really good. Allison immediately volunteered to go to a nearby convenience store to get some. Unbeknownst to her, Truman followed her out the door. As Allison began to back out of the driveway she heard a terrible yelp. Truman had crossed paths behind her and got caught in the undercarriage of the car. Luckily he broke no bones, but his front legs were mangled, leaving them swollen and badly bruised. He spent the next two days in bed, not wanting to move or do much of anything. Clearly, he was in great pain.

Truman recovered from his injuries rather quickly. What was surprising, however, was that as his front legs healed, his back legs improved as well. Because Cushing's Disease deteriorated the joints in his back legs, Truman had become more and more dependent on his front legs to help him walk. That is why he limped. That is also why he lost strength in his back leg muscles. When his front legs were injured, he was once again forced to rely on his back legs. The muscles and joints soon became stronger. While he still moves slowly, Truman is now walking with a steady gait and no limp. With each passing day he continues to grow sturdier and more stable.

The moral of this story is that adversity can and should make you stronger. When bad things happen, do you put your head down and start limping, as you wallow in misery and self pity? Or do adversity and misfortune provide you with opportunities? When things get painful or don't go our way, we have a choice. We can limp, wallow and whimper, or we can drag our tired and aching body off the ground, stand tall and move steadily forward.

Any corporation that has been around for a number of years tends to develop a culture. This culture becomes part of its identity and its trademark. The best and most successful companies have a culture that is defined by the belief that they can overcome almost any obstacle. This is accomplished through hard work, teamwork and an unwavering desire to rise to any challenge.

Today my dog is stronger and healthier than he was a month ago. Misfortune and adversity didn't make him so. Overcoming it did. Can you say the same thing about yourself, your job and your company? There are always struggles, difficulties and pain. Success comes when you stand tall, move forward and resolve to emerge from difficult times stronger and steadier than ever before.

A DUTY AND AN HONOR TO SERVE

It wasn't planned that way, but I find it both ironic and appropriate that Election Day and Veteran's Day fall so closely together on the calendar. Once you get past the flag waving, saber rattling, mudslinging, rhetoric and slogans, both days represent a call to service and a duty to serve with honor.

Once upon a time, politicians were referred to as public servants. They still are public servants, but are generally called any number of less polite names. Some of the contempt that we have for our elected officials is deserved. Much of it is not. Most of these individuals are successful pro-fessionals who have chosen to expand their role in the community, to offer their skills and expertise toward improving the greater good. As a rule, the hours are long, the pay is hardly exceptional, and you become a moving target for anyone with even the most minor reason to disagree with you. Why then would anyone do it? Is it ego or insanity? A little of both probably helps, but mostly it is neither.

I believe that most elected officials enter office with a genuine desire to improve their communities and their country. They do this by offering ideas and solutions to some very complex problems. They have achieved some degree of personal success and wealth, and now wish to help elevate the standard of living and the quality of life for others. We may disagree with them, but their willingness to serve and their honest intent are indeed worthy of our respect and admiration.

While I have never been on a ballot (except once when I entered a protest vote by writing in my own name), I have also never missed an opportunity to vote. I have cast my ballot in every election since 1977. Most of these votes were immediately negated by an opposing ballot from my wife. Whom we voted for was of little significance compared to the importance of fulfilling our role in the process.

Veteran's Day has a more personal significance to me. The four years that I spent in the military were hardly heroic or even noteworthy, but it was indeed an honor to serve. Like most veterans, I didn't join as an act of patriotism. I joined to escape difficult times. Jobs were scarce and my family life was not good. It is a common story. For four years I proudly served. Yet by offering my service, I received much more in return. Virtually every veteran I know continues to serve others in some way or another. We consider it an honor and an obligation to do so. We understand what our country has given us and know the importance of giving back. We all have a duty to give back.

The vast majority of citizens in our communities are neither veterans nor elected officials. They are simply everyday hard working people who are trying to do the best job they can, both at work and at home. Yet every one of us, from the student, to the factory worker, to the corporate executive, to the war hero, continues to have an obligation to help others. As long as there are others who are less fortunate than we are, that duty will not go away.

Service doesn't have to come via the military or elected office. You can participate in a charity event. You can mentor or tutor. You can visit a nursing home. Just offer a kind word and a helping hand to a stranger. It doesn't have to cost money or take very much time. None of us would hesitate to help a friend in need. Why not help others we do not yet know? If we all take a moment to count our blessings, we will understand just how fortunate we are in so many ways. Why not share that good fortune? Give a little bit back.

Despite my own tendency to criticize, I am very grateful to our elected officials for their willingness to serve. I am even more grateful to our veterans and our active duty servicemen and servicewomen for their great sacrifices. They have all served with duty, honor and dignity. If they can serve, so can we. Make a little time for someone else. Fulfill your obligation.

A FEW THOUGHTS ON DIVERSITY

Diversity. For the past ten years or more it has been a major buzzword in corporate America. Some companies struggle with it, developing programs and mandates to establish a bias-free environment. Other businesses have no issue, as they have always maintained a culture of inclusiveness. For inclusive employers it is an easy approach. If you have skill, talent, drive and ethics, they want you. It doesn't matter if you are black, white, Asian, Hispanic, homosexual, heterosexual, disabled, Catholic, Muslim, Jewish, Mormon, atheist, overweight, underweight, old, young, male, female, conservative, liberal or undecided. It just doesn't matter. If you can do the job and work as a team, these businesses want you. The best companies in America are the ones that learned long ago that their employees should be as diverse as the customers they serve. It's good ethics. It's good business.

I've been thinking a lot about diversity lately. The term used to apply primarily to race, but lately it has come to mean almost any characteristic that makes us unique and different. Diversity is a very good thing, but it can be scary and challenging. Our race, gender and spirituality, along with other characteristics shape who we are and how we look at the world. At their best, our beliefs and characteristics make us empathetic and considerate towards others who are different. At their worst, they make us closed-minded, paranoid and prejudiced. It can be scary to be around people who are very different than us. It can also be a wonderful experience to get to know people who can broaden our horizons and share their experiences. It all comes down to how you look at it. Is it an opportunity or a challenge? I view it as an opportunity. Consider the following:

Key West, Florida. This tiny tourist town is two miles wide by four miles long. It has a year-round population of about 22,000 residents. Crammed into its borders you will find a U.S. Navy air base, a large gay community and a row of mansions that are owned by celebrities and wealthy business tycoons. You will find poverty in a Caribbean village made up mostly of Cuban, Bahamian and Haitian immigrants. There are several large churches and active religious organizations. What makes Key West unique, however, isn't its diversity. Many small cities have most of these characteristics. What makes Key West different is the level of tolerance. The poor immigrant and the wealthy celebrity are treated as equals. The military hero and the radical expatriate are respected and valued. In Key West, intolerance is not tolerated.

The Olympics. Every few years the nations of the world put aside their differences and come together, using athletic competition as a means to celebrate the diversity of our planet. Each athlete represents an entire nation. The beauty of the Olympics is not who wins the most gold medals or what world records will be broken. It is the purity of sport and the belief that athletics can bring countries together in a divisive world. It is the stories of triumph—of individuals who have overcome immense odds and faced daunting challenges, just for the chance to participate. The Olympics are all about diversity.

The mentally and physically challenged. Until very recently I did not include this group in my picture of diversity. But if we are truly inclusive, these individuals must be given the same respect and opportunities as others. While these persons may have limitations, they also have the capacity to work hard and lead productive lives. More and more companies are realizing the value that goes with reaching out to this great untapped resource. Reasonable accommodations often lead to extraordinary results.

All employees want to take pride in the company they work for. How you run your business is just as important as the money you earn and the jobs that are created. Diversity should be part of the solution, not a problem to overcome. Let us celebrate our differences and enjoy the opportunity to surround ourselves with coworkers who are every bit as diverse as the world around us. It is the right way to work. It is the right way to live.

A SAILOR'S STORY

When I think of the few great loves in my life, it is only natural that family and friends immediately come to mind, along with a few special places that I have visited and lived. Likewise, I can't help but think of the USS Shenandoah, a rusty old repair ship that was my home during the late 1970s. Once the pride of the fleet, by the time I arrived on board her best days were clearly behind her. Thirty-five years of service through three major wars had taken their toll. Through it all, the old gal had a charm and spirit that few could match.

In the post Vietnam years of 1978 and 1979 the country had fallen on hard times. The scars from that war had not healed and the military was not viewed in high favor. That sentiment was coupled with one of the toughest economic downturns in history. Unemployment was high, inflation was high, and the budget deficit was high. To help trim expenses during this brief time of peace, Congress deeply cut defense spending. Budgets were slashed. Older ships like the Shenandoah were either decommissioned or allowed to fall into disrepair. That made our jobs more difficult, but it did nothing to kill morale.

Back then, I worked as a machinist. Not a very good one, I must admit, but a machinist nonetheless. I was in Repair Division, Shop 31-A, where we repaired and rebuilt pumps and valves to keep our ship and others seaworthy. Proudly displayed on the starboard bulkhead was a large poster that proclaimed our resolve. "We have done so much, with so little, for so long, that we can now do anything with nothing." The sign said it. We believed it. We lived it.

In the spring and summer of 1979, the Shenandoah made her final voyage, traveling to the Mediterranean Sea for six months. There we tended to Sixth Fleet ships that were serving abroad. In early June we steamed into the Bay of Naples, along the southwest coast of Italy. Directly across the harbor from us rose the infamous Mount Vesuvius, a smoldering 3,800-foot tall active volcano. At the first sight of it, I immediately turned to my shipmate and closest friend Jack D'Orio, and proclaimed, "We are going to climb that hill." Jack simply looked back at me in total disbelief. Four weeks later, we stood on its summit.

We could have done it the easy way, but there was no pride or challenge in that. For a few cents, a gondola would have taken us from the base to the rim. Instead, we loaded backpacks with food and water and began climbing from the opposite side of the mountain. Following paths through several vineyards and a small forest, we quickly ascended. It was a warm, dry day with a slight breeze. The two of us were reasonably fit. It took us only four hours to rise 3,000 feet towards our goal. It would take another four hours to reach the top.

At about the 3,000-foot mark all vegetation disappeared. It was there that the mountain rose up at a much sharper angle and our once firm footing was replaced by rocks, gravel and loose volcanic ash. The sun beat down hard, while a steady breeze blew dust and ash around us, making it difficult to see and breathe. We continued onward and upward. For every four steps we took, we slid three steps back. We were tired and dirty and starting to wonder if we had made a wise decision. At that point there were only two choices. We could see it through, or we could turn back, while seemingly so close to our goal. Again, we set our sights upward.

The last 100 feet were by far the most difficult. There the wind became stronger, and the terrain even more hostile as the summit turned up at perhaps a 50- or 60- degree angle. We spent the last hour of our climb literally clawing our way on our hands and knees. Finally, at 4 p.m. on July 7, 1979, we stood on the top of the mountain. There, my good friend and I shared a victory bottle of wine before taking the gondola and train back to the ship we called home.

The political and economic struggles that have occurred in recent years remind me in many ways of those days in the late 1970s. Specifics and circumstances may be different, but there are numerous similarities. Once again, the country is faced with a prolonged period of political and social unrest. More significantly, businesses are confronted with various hardships and logistical challenges that are forcing them to make difficult and at times extremely unpopular decisions. Few if any companies are immune to this. The obvious end result is that any business's collective morale takes a pretty hard hit when faced with budget cuts, payroll reductions and operational changes. But though morale may take a hit, resolve and determination must never wane.

Companies repeatedly ask their employees to do the impossible, and almost without fail, employees find a way to deliver. Like the old poster from my sailor days, all across the economic landscape you will find businesses that are doing so much with so little that they are now convinced they can accomplish almost anything. It is that kind of resolve that can turn low morale into grit and determination. Look for it. Embrace it. Cherish it. Foster it. Cultivate it. Harvest it. And never take it for granted.

ARE YOU TOO GOOD TO SWEEP FLOORS?

My daughter Emily has had some great summer jobs. While in high school, she sat people on a roller coaster at a Six Flags Amusement Park. In college, she worked the beer cart for a local golf course. I was never so lucky. I mixed cement for my grandfather, using a shovel, a hoe and a wheelbarrow. I also worked with the janitors at my high school, and later washed dishes for a local steakhouse. Several of my friends shoveled horse manure at the stables at the nearby Monmouth Park Racetrack. By comparison, doing dishes or mixing cement didn't seem so bad. Hard, sometimes dirty work has never bothered me. It is good, honest labor.

I was recently talking with a friend about our summer jobs. Kevin tells the story of how after graduating from high school he took a job at a supermarket in Maine before going off to college. On his first day of work, the store manager handed him a broom and told him to sweep the sales floor. When he finished that, he was to sweep the stockroom floor, clean the restrooms, then return to the sales floor and sweep it again. After finishing that, he was to see the store manager to ensure that these tasks were properly done. A bit indignant and in mild protest, Kevin complained. "But sir, I'm a college student." The store manager seized the broom and the moment. "Oh, I'm sorry. My mistake. Here, let me first show you how to sweep a floor."

Are you too good to sweep floors, clean bathrooms or wash windows? I'm not. We all have to do our share of dirty work. Someone has to do it. If you are a parent, you know all about changing diapers, cleaning spills and handling assorted unmentionable mishaps. You do it because it has to be done. You do it because as a parent that is your job. Why should it be any different when you come to work?

None of us should ever feel we are too good to perform any task simply because it is dirty, boring, repetitive, malodorous or in some other way unpleasant. Always consider the fact that someone has to do that job. Consider the possible consequences if that job didn't get done. Are you willing to say to a coworker, "I don't have to do that job because I am better than you"? I certainly hope not.

Numerous studies have shown that both clients and employees alike will judge the quality of a business on the cleanliness of its offices, restrooms, and other facilities. Cleaning the restroom or sweeping a floor might seem menial or insignificant, but it can have a very real impact on the success or failure of a business. CNO. Clean. Neat. Organized. It is a part of customer service. It is a part of putting forward the best overall image to your prospective clients and customers. If you're in the business of selling health care products, your customers expect you to work within a healthy environment. If you are in the auditing and accounting business, a neat and organized office creates the impression of careful, accurate work. If you are in manufacturing, CNO means precision.

I say it often and I'll continue to say it: we all have the same job. Regardless of whether you are a corporate president or a mailroom clerk, your job is to help make the company you work for operate as smoothly and successfully as possible. That may include operations planning, or sales, or maintenance, or it may include sweeping floors and cleaning restrooms. It is everyone's job. It is what customers and clients want, expect and deserve. If I can do it (and I do), so can you. No one is too good to sweep floors.

BEFORE WE JUMP TO CONCLUSIONS...

One of the few good things about visiting a doctor or dentist's office is that you are inclined to pick up and read outdated magazine articles about a variety of topics that you would otherwise never consider. One time, while confined to my doctor's waiting room, I found myself reading a piece about tigers. The author of the article claimed that no two tigers have the exact same stripe patterns on their faces. This is for identification purposes. This is how tigers can tell each other apart.

I finished the article and thought for a moment. Then I shook my head in disbelief. Thousands of people will read this article and never question the content, but how accurate could it possibly be? There are thousands of tigers. Has each and every one been identified and had its face mapped? Has anyone ever sat down with a tiger and had a lengthy conversation about the identification process? If so, I would like to meet this person. How do we know the stripes are for identification? Maybe the stripes are for camouflage, or to attract a mate. Perhaps tigers recognize each other by scent, or purring sounds, or eye contact. Maybe the stripes serve no purpose at all.

I am reasonably sure that the article was thoroughly researched. The conclusion may well be correct. I simply have a problem with someone passing off an intelligent guess as being a matter of true fact. Scientists, anthropologists, and historians do this all of the time. So do businesses.

Some years ago, I was talking with a corporate executive, whom I have to believe did not think too highly of me. He asked if I was a sports fan. I told him indeed I was. I am a rather avid baseball fan at that. He then asked if I ever record games and watch them later if I'm unable to get to a television when the game is on. I replied no. In such a case I would simply read about it the following day in the newspaper. To that he answered, "That is why you will never be successful. You let other people tell you what is going on, rather than seeing it for yourself." His criticism of me may have been valid, but it certainly had nothing to do with whether or not I recorded baseball games.

Quick conclusions and snap judgments happen all the time. When an American car manufacturer is down in sales you will hear hundreds of reasons why. Foreign competition coupled with a weak economy and an undervalued dollar. High unemployment. Over-regulation. Gas prices.

Questionable quality. Poor marketing. Any or all of those factors may come in to play, or it may be none of the above. We think we know, but do we really?

The reasons for success are equally as abstract. When a retail unit posts a strong increase in sales and profit, particularly in a tight market, the store manager is apt to get considerable credit and praise. But was the success really to his or her credit? A strong staff and the demise of a nearby competitor may have made all the difference. Sometimes it is leadership, planning, and execution. Other times it is simply dumb luck and good fortune. Sometimes success comes because of us, while other times it is in spite of us. If it is skill, then the success should be duplicated over several years. If it is luck, then it will probably be a one-hit wonder.

My point is that we should never settle for the quick answer, the conventional wisdom, or the status quo. You always have to dig deeper. Even then, you can never be sure that you have drawn the correct conclusion. Make intelligent guesses, but be flexible enough to know that you may have to adjust to changing information and observations.

DO YOU HAVE A JOB OR A CAREER?

A few years ago, I had the unavoidable pleasure of turning 50 years old. It's really not such a painful milestone. I have my health, a great family, and some wonderful friends. I also have a good steady job that I have been doing for a very long time. Since passing the half-century mark, I have been thinking a bit more about retirement. Over the years, I have seen a number of family members, friends and coworkers decide that it was time to turn in their keys and do something else. Soon it will be my turn.

At my current job, I can retire once I have reached the combination of 25 years of service and 55 years of age. There is no mandatory retirement age, and a significant number of coworkers have stayed on for 40 or even 50-plus years. As I close in on my own eligibility, I find myself wondering: will I retire as soon as possible or will I stay for many years to come? Fifty-five is not that old. I could easily log another 20 more years, assuming my health is good and my bosses still want me.

A short while ago, my wife and I sat down over a cup of coffee and discussed some of our future plans. Both of our daughters are now in college. Empty nest. Diane and I have been very fortunate. When the girls were young, we were able to make the decision that one of us would be the primary source of income, while the other would be home as much as possible for the kids. It is a decision that not every family can afford to make. As I have said, we are very fortunate, and we know it. Diane has worked part-time and per diem for most of the past twenty years. She is now ready to work full-time again. In discussing our future plans, she commented, "I have had jobs. You have had a career. I want a career."

Do you have a job, or is it a career? What is the difference? Is there a difference? The Webster's New Collegiate Dictionary defines a job as: work that is for hire for a given service or period. In contrast, a career is a profession for which one trains and which is undertaken as a permanent calling.

For me, what started as a job became a career. I took a job with this company after graduating from college, and then worked hard to advance to a level that has provided me with both means and satisfaction. It is now my permanent calling. But it is important to understand that one need not be a manager, executive, or some well-educated professional to have a career. A mail clerk, plumber, cashier, or food service worker may also have a career. It is not defined by education, job title or salary. Careers are based on a sense of loyalty, pride, and a commitment to excellence. Those characteristics will help guide you in determining if it is indeed your life's calling.

Do you go to work just to collect your pay? If so, that's okay. Many employees who fit this description work very hard, stay at one job for a very long time, and are a vital part of the team. Maybe your current job is just a temporary piece of a greater puzzle. It provides money to help pay for school, or to supplement your family's income, or to reduce debts or save for a large purchase. That's okay, too. On the other hand, if you have been at your job for several years and find that you actually enjoy coming to work, like to work hard and assume responsibilities, and have no thoughts of leaving anytime soon, then you may be heading towards a career.

By definition, your company gave you a job, but you have the choice as to whether or not it becomes a career. If you already have made that decision, I suspect you find both pride and comfort in the sense of certainty it provides. Maybe you like your job, but are unsure if it fits the description of a "permanent calling." No problem. There is no paperwork to fill out in order to turn your job into a career. Keep working hard, keep learning and keep striving to get ahead. Before too long, you too may be thinking about retirement. When that day comes, I hope you can say, "I chose wisely. I had a great career." I know I can.

DO YOU PLAY TO WIN OR ARE YOU JUST TRYING NOT TO LOSE?

Athletes hear this said from time to time. It's a close game. The opponent is really tough. You have a lead. A slim lead. You just want to hang on long enough to get the win. What do you do? You go from being aggressive and offensive-minded, to overly cautious. You do whatever it takes to tick seconds off the clock without making that costly mistake. You guard the ball extra carefully. You run the slowest and safest plays possible. You stop playing offense. You work really hard at not losing.

The problem with this strategy is that it usually doesn't work. You built your lead by being aggressive and daring. You earned the right to win because you continued to charge forward. You challenged your opponent on every play. The reason you are winning is because you are playing to win. To change that strategy just because victory is within reach makes no sense at all. I can guarantee that your opponents are not playing it safe. They know they are losing, so they are doing everything within their power to break you. They are playing twice as hard. They are taking risks. They are exploiting your caution.

A while ago I saw an interview with a top executive at Federal Express. His company has had moderate success in taking on the U.S. Postal Service, proving that it can provide many of the same services, with greater quality, efficiency and profitability. Many people believe that government-run operations tend to be less efficient than their private sector counterparts. Federal Express has helped to prove this point. This shortcoming is not due to any innate plan to be wasteful or laden with red tape. It is quite the contrary. The U.S. government is organized and designed to avoid making mistakes. This is most admirable. They have all sorts of checks and balances to ensure that things are done uniformly and consistently. Day-to-day operations tend to be very precise, very predictable, very ethical, and very safe. The government plays to avoid losing.

Businesses, however, succeed by taking risks and learning from mistakes. They are constantly reacting to change and trying new things. Because they make mistakes, they learn faster and adapt quicker. This makes them leaner and more efficient. Businesses also have the burden of competition. Every business has competitors who are trying to steal their customers and market share by doing things faster and cheaper than anyone else. The companies that enjoy the greatest success are those that take intelligent risks, then adapt quickly as situations change. These companies know how to play to win.

While competition may be the primary challenge facing businesses, change can be the most daunting and unpredictable. The economy is in constant change. So are demographics. There may be new environmental concerns and regulatory procedures to consider. If you are playing not to lose, you proceed slowly and cautiously. If you are playing to win, you embrace and attack these changes, not with reckless abandon, but with an aggressive pursuit of opportunities.

I don't think it will surprise too many people if we see more and more private businesses taking on roles that were previously relegated to the government. The government's approach of safety and success is admirable and ideally suited for certain tasks and agencies. Others need to be more efficient. When greater efficiency is the attainable goal, and in particular, when it is achieved, we all play to win and no one is the loser.

DO YOU REMEMBER THAT GREAT SOFA YOU BOUGHT? I DIDN'T THINK SO.

Those who know me best know that I live a fairly modest life. I have an average house in a quiet and unpretentious New England town. I drive an average car that has well over 100,000 miles on it. I dress well for my job but am otherwise more comfortable wearing jeans and a baseball jersey. We all want to be comfortable and own a few nice things, but the stuff just isn't that important to me. I would much rather do than have.

I was reminded of this lack of materialism last November when my daughter asked me what we were doing for Veteran's Day. The question might seem a bit odd, but it isn't. It's a holiday that I like to celebrate. While my service in the military was hardly noteworthy, I take great pride in being a part of that exclusive group of men and women who have spent time in the armed forces. Often I will take a day off from work and go on a day trip. In past years, I have taken my daughters and their boyfriends to Cooperstown, New York, to visit the Baseball Hall of Fame. Other times, my wife and I have gone to Boston for the day or spent an afternoon at Mystic Seaport. When I told my daughter that I really had no plans for Veteran's Day, she immediately became concerned. "You have to go somewhere," she said. "It's a tradition." I was surprised at how important it was to her. We have a number of family traditions. Sometimes I underestimate how valuable these rituals are.

We all know people who are constantly saving to buy something fancy. A big house. An expensive car. Fancy clothes. Big screen-televisions. Jewelry. Most of their money goes towards paying for the expensive stuff that they buy. Status symbols. The stuff gives them pleasure, but they never really do anything or go anywhere. Maybe you are one of these people. I have no right to criticize how anyone else lives, but I just don't get it. Owning stuff is nice, but owning a great experience or a great memory seems much more valuable to me.

And what of your job? We work hard to earn money so we can afford to buy stuff. We also work hard to afford the vacation or the big holiday gathering. Work provides us with income and a sense of community. It gives us experiences and it can give us joy. The one thing it should never do is replace our family and friends. Work gives us the means to enjoy other things but it should never be so consuming that we ignore the things and people that matter most.

The true value of something is often measured in how long it lasts. Twenty years from now, while you are sitting around with friends and family, will you be talking about that great sofa or dinette set that you bought years ago? Will you be talking about how hard you had to work to save up and pay for it? Probably not. It is far more likely your memories and conversations will be of a great vacation or a holiday family gathering or of a special moment with your spouse, children or siblings. So, which is more valuable? Which lasts longer? Which experience is ultimately more satisfying?

Nothing is more important or more valuable than sharing time with the people you love. Shared experiences are the richest of treasures. Pick your own holiday and rejoice in it. I'm not sure what I will be doing this year for Veteran's Day, but I will surely do my best to make it memorable.

EVERYBODY'S TALKING, BUT NOT TO YOU.

Don't you just hate it when you find out that someone has been talking about you behind your back? I'll bet you do, but almost everybody does it. It's a natural part of conversation to talk to others about friends, relatives, colleagues and coworkers. It is only perceived as talking behind the back when negative things are said. No one ever complains when they learn that someone else has complimented them.

We all have traits and habits that grate on other people. Some of these traits can be annoying while others are amusing. There is the person who is always early or late. There is also the person who is always in a panic or the one who is so laid-back that nothing seems important to him or her. Often this will result in some good-natured kidding. "Mary has her own time zone." Or "Hey Mike, it's strictly decaf for you today." In these cases, it is not uncommon for the persons involved to know they have this particular shortcoming, and as long as the comments are not malicious, it's all in good fun.

Some subjects are not so easy to broach without being perceived as personal attacks. Yet people do talk about and judge us on a number of characteristics, including some that are a bit sensitive in nature. To avoid being viewed in a negative light, and to avoid being fodder for other people's conversations, there are a few tendencies we should all make an effort to avoid.

Stinky syndrome. We have all encountered coworkers who for whatever reason seem to emit an unpleasant body odor. Usually, this is not a matter of personal hygiene, but rather a function of diet and body chemistry. There is no gentle way to approach this subject with someone and have it seem polite. The best you might do is to suggest a brand of cologne you like. This, too, may become a problem when a person falls in love with a fragrance and douses with it. Too much of a good thing is bad. Too much cologne fills a room, sucks out all the air and becomes worse than any odor it may be trying to mask.

Stinky syndrome, part 2. Bad breath. Most people practice good oral hygiene, but as the saying goes, you are what you eat. Garlic, onions, coffee and tobacco are notorious for showing up on your breath. Pungent spices and seasonings should be avoided around lunch time, particularly if you know you will be interacting with others afterwards. Smokers and coffee drinkers should keep breath mints handy at all times. If you are talking with someone and little by little the distance between you increases, it may be a sign that you need another mint. Or it could mean...

Close talking. Assuming your breath is fine, and your body odor is in check, if coworkers are increasing their distance at small intervals, it may be a sign that you are standing too close to them. People like to have a bit of room between themselves and the person they are interacting with. While there are no clear rules on distance, close talkers tend to move too near and violate the other person's comfort zone. Everyone needs his or her own space. Respect that.

Loud talking. I tend to talk too loud on the phone. I know this and have to consciously try to keep my voice down. As I become more excited or enthusiastic, my volume goes up. Others we encounter always have their volume set on high. Their normal conversations can be heard by everyone in the room, and in some cases in the next city. It could be that the person is hard of hearing, but more than likely they are just trying too hard to be heard.

Wimpy shakes. Soft hands are nice. Limp, weak, clammy handshakes are not. A handshake is a greeting, or a means of locking down an agreement. In both cases it should be done with confidence. A firm, not bone-crushing handshake, while briefly making eye contact is a pleasant and simple way to connect with others. Some people have handshakes that feel like a piece of raw fish. You will not find much confidence instilled there. Eye contact is important too. You should, however, avoid...

The stare and glare. Eye contact is good but not all the time. Staring is creepy. When talking to others you want to make good eye contact but you also need to avert your glance from time to time. You want to connect with the person, not burn a hole into their soul.

People are talking about you. Be aware of yourself. Don't over-think these things, but be knowledgeable of your own habits and tendencies. If you ask, a close friend may be willing to tell you what some of those annoying traits are. If not, keep it simple. Practice good hygiene and always be respectful of others in your daily interactions. Others will continue to talk, so you should try to give them only good things to say.

EVERYTHING I KNOW ABOUT MANAGING I LEARNED FROM MY KIDS

I like to tell people that I learned more from five minutes in the Navy than I did in four years of college. This may be true, but it doesn't nearly compare to what I have learned in the process of raising two daughters. It's not easy to be a good parent. It's also not easy being a good manager. I would like to think that I have gotten pretty good at both, but it surely was not always that way. Newborn through the age of four were tough years. I'm not good with babies. They don't speak English. They cry all the time. You have to carry them everywhere. Then there is the diaper issue... My first few years as a dad were rough. My first few years as a manager weren't exactly smooth either. I knew how to work hard, but I still had a lot to learn about managing people. Fortunately, I had my kids to teach me.

Everything I know about managing people, I learned from my kids. I guess what I am trying to say is that many of the skills that go into being a good parent are easily applied to other aspects of our lives. In my case, I have repeatedly found that much of what I have learned from my daughters has helped me in how I approach situations at work. This is not just specific to managing, but to almost any day-to-day issue or problem. Here are a few lessons that Emily and Allison have taught me:

Look and listen. If you really want to know what's going on, just pretend to be invisible and keep your eyes and ears open. Or ask a simple question and let the other person talk for as long as they want. You may not get what you want to hear, but you will probably hear what you need to know.

Every problem is not a crisis. Don't overreact to every little bump in the road. There will be plenty of big problems to tackle. Do react to little problems so they don't grow into a crisis. Just try not to freak out over every little thing.

Never underestimate the power of enthusiasm. Ability is great, but passion and enthusiasm can accomplish much more than any skill. If you don't believe me, go to the beach and watch a group of kids building a sand castle.

Celebrate success. Forgive mistakes. Some days you are going to be proud. Other times you will be disappointed. Enjoy the good times. Learn from the hard times. Then move on. Never hold a grudge.

Just because you disagree with someone doesn't mean they are wrong. This applies particularly well when dealing with teenagers and bosses. No two people think exactly alike. Keep an open mind when encountering a difference of opinion. You just might learn something from an opposing point of view that will change your mind.

Yelling never accomplishes anything. If you are yelling, it is a safe bet that the other person isn't listening. Speaking in a calm and civil tone is far more likely to get the message across and achieve the desired results.

Never talk down to people. Everyone, regardless of their age, education, job or personal characteristics, deserves to be treated with fairness and respect. When you talk down to people you make yourself look like a bully and a fool.

The more you teach, the more you learn. Share your knowledge and experiences. Encourage questions. You will not know the answers to many of the questions you get. Then it is your turn to find out and learn.

Trust people. I have tried to avoid giving my kids too many rules. I give them values, and then trust them to do the right thing. When a problem arises we address it. I also try not to over-manage. I would rather allow people the freedom to show the world what they can do. Sometimes I am amazed and impressed. When I am not, I get to teach.

Show appreciation. Children want to know that they are loved, they are appreciated, and they are safe. Coworkers are not much different. We all want to know that our efforts are valued, valuable and never taken for granted.

That's a 10-step lesson in how to be a successful manager, courtesy of my kids. If you have kids or are somebody's kid, you can probably add another dozen or more items to the list. The important thing to realize is that these are not just lessons and guidelines for the workplace. They apply and translate very well into almost every other aspect of daily life.

FIVE MISTAKES EVERY-
ONE SHOULD MAKE

The above title comes from an online article I saw in Real Simple Magazine. Real Simple. I like that. Everything is so complicated these days. It is widely accepted that the best way to solve any complex problem is to break it down into a series of smaller and simpler parts, then solve them one by one. Unfortunately, we all make mistakes...even when addressing simple problems. To err is human, but not all mistakes are created equal. Some blunders can actually be good. A good mistake can teach, motivate, inspire, warn, and if nothing else be cause for a good self-deprecating laugh. Here is my take on the Real Simple five that everyone should make:

1. Totally Embarrass Yourself. This is easy to do. Did you ever get dressed for work without being totally awake and put on a pair of socks that were inside out or didn't match? Perhaps you got tongue-tied while trying to make an important point, or worse yet, said hello to someone by calling them the wrong name. We all have these embarrassing moments. They are good. They remind others that we are just as human as they are, while giving us the opportunity to laugh at ourselves. None of us should ever take ourselves too seriously.

2. Ruffle Other People's Feathers. Obviously there are limits and cautions that go with this one. There is a fine line between feather ruffling and being disrespectful or infuriating. It is easy to compromise your own standards when you are trying to impress others. There need to be limits to this. Let others know that while you are indeed a team player, you are also not a pushover. Take a stand on an unpopular issue. Speak your mind. While others may find it disagreeable, they should at least respect you for your honesty and commitment.

3. Follow Trends Blindly. This is good business at its imperfect best. It is impossible to know when a fad or trend will become a permanent part of our culture; therefore, fads must be treated with enthusiasm and respect. You can guess, but most of the time your predictions will be wrong. I was one of those people who thought disco would last forever

but rap music was just a passing fad. It is far better to over-embrace a fad than to miss out on a genuine cultural phenomenon.

4. Be Willing to Fail at Something You Love. It is easy to throw yourself passionately at a job, hobby, sport or skill that you love. That doesn't mean you will be any good at it. Golfers, skiers, and fishermen understand this quite well. If it gives you joy, then a few rare moments of success will make it well-worth enduring the countless days of failure.

5. Carelessly Put Yourself at Risk. This doesn't mean that you physically put yourself in dangerous situations. Go with a hunch. Play a long shot. Logic and reason may be completely against you, but we should never underestimate the value of instinct and intuition. You may not want to bet the house, but a good hunch is often worth more than a safe, reliable plan.

That's the Real Simple Five. I'm not sure that any of the five are mistakes. I think it is more about being true to oneself. It is about taking control and responsibility for your job, your actions, your destiny and your life. How can that be considered a blunder?

HOW TO WORK REALLY, REALLY HARD AND STILL NOT ACCOMPLISH VERY MUCH

There is an often used and over-quoted adage which warns us that "effort does not always equal results." Unfortunately, the cliché happens to be true. That is not to say that laziness will get you very far either, but it is safe to say that the hardest-working people in any job are not necessarily the ones who get the most accomplished. Why is this? There are many reasons...

I am most inclined to think that the primary reason why some people accomplish less than others, despite great effort, is because they fall into a series of work routine traps that make them less productive than they could be. Here are six common pitfalls that should be avoided whenever possible:

1. Winging it. Lately, the days have been quite unpredictable, so why bother making a list? More will get done if you let the day come to you and make progress as the workday develops. Wrong, wrong, wrong. Staying organized is the most important thing you can do and the one sure way to get things accomplished. Every workday should begin with a list of things to be done. Every workday should end with a few notes and reminders of what needs to be done tomorrow. As the day progresses, new items will be added to the list. Some tasks will be completed and some rendered irrelevant, while others will be put off for future lists. The list is what keeps you organized and on track. It is also what will give you a sense of accomplishment as you cross off the many items that are completed.

2. Do all the tough jobs first. This is one of those times when something seems to make sense, but really doesn't. If you do all of the difficult jobs first, a lot of little yet very important tasks will not get done. While it is necessary to tackle the toughest assignments, they can be unpredictable and time-consuming. You should spend some time on a big project, and then offset it with a couple of smaller, easier tasks. In the end, you will have a smoother and more productive day. Both large and small projects are important. Balancing them is the key.

3. Work through lunch. Sometimes this is needed, but it shouldn't be an everyday thing. In the course of daily routines, it is important to give yourself a break. Get some fresh air. Grab a bite to eat. Read a newspaper. In short, clear your head and recharge your energy level. A much needed break will improve your brainpower, productivity and attitude.

4. Focus on what you are good at. This is an easy trap to fall into. We like to do the things we are good at. When we do things that make use of the best of our abilities, we are bound to be productive. While this is true, it also limits our potential. Don't assume that you are not good at something simply because you tried it once and struggled. Learn new tasks and skills. You may not be good right away, but you will quickly expand the scope of your abilities. This will lead to greater results.

5. Don't ask questions. Nobody wants to appear to be dumb or incompetent. If you ask too many questions, people may think you don't know what you are doing. Wrong. If you don't ask questions, then mess up a job, people will begin to question your ability and judgment. Smart people ask a lot of questions. It doesn't matter if you have been on the job for twenty minutes or twenty years. The more questions you ask, the more you learn, understand and can accomplish.

6. Do it yourself. We have all heard the saying "If you want something done right, you have to do it yourself." Wrong. Businesses are built on teams and teamwork. Share the responsibility and share the success. Employees and in particular managers who take on too many tasks alone, accomplish far less than team players. Shouldering too much of the burden leads to low morale, fatigue, and ultimately failure.

We all work very hard. We do our best because we take pride in our work. We care about our company and our coworkers. We enjoy being productive. Let's try to avoid the traps that can limit this. Let's see our effort be equaled or exceeded by our results.

"I MAY BE DIFFERENT, BUT I'M NOT STUPID!"

Three stories.

As a sailor aboard the USS Shenandoah, I became good friends with a shipmate named Rick Hodges. On the surface it was an odd pairing. I was a street-smart kid from Northern New Jersey. Rick was a country boy from Leaksville, Mississippi. I would talk fast and tell tales of the bright lights of New York City. Rick spoke in a slow drawl and would talk about growing up on a farm in the Deep South.

One of the things that surprised me most about my friend was that despite my misconceptions about Southern racism, Rick had as many black friends as white. I remember asking him about this once. Rick simply smiled and put his arm on my shoulder. "Raaalph," he drawled, "I reckon most people up north believe us Southern white boys are all a bunch of racist rednecks who drive beat-up pickup trucks, spit tobacco juice and have Confederate flag tattoos on our arms. I s'pose some of us do, but most of us don't. Truth is that most of us are just like everyone else. I've met just as many racists from the North as I know from the South."

Ali worked for me as an assistant several years ago. He came to this country from the Middle East and got a finance degree from a major American university. As soon as he was eligible, Ali became a U.S. citizen. I always found him to be an interesting and engaging individual, who worked hard but also had a delightful sense of humor. The one problem we had was that Ali spoke with a fairly thick accent which made him, at times, difficult to understand. When that happened, I simply asked him to slow down and separate his words so I could grasp what he was saying. It was no big deal. He knew he had an accent and was trying to improve his language skills. Ali was eventually transferred elsewhere. One day his boss called me to complain. "What is wrong with this guy? He is soooo stupid. How did you work with him? I can't understand a word he says." Ali was anything but stupid, but his supervisor mistook his accent to be a sign of ignorance. In truth, it was Ali's boss who was ignorant.

Jen was a clerk who worked for me for about a year. She was bright, enthusiastic, and eternally optimistic. Jen was also paralyzed on most of her left side and struggled to walk using a cane. She had cerebral palsy. Jen was easy to understand, but when she spoke, her words were often slurred. She later moved to Michigan, but for a while she was one of my best employees. I would often watch with dismay as others would become frustrated with her as she struggled to coordinate her one good arm with the other. Even worse was when someone would talk to her in a really loud voice as though her disability had somehow made her deaf as well as crippled. Then there were those who would talk down to her as though she was a two-year-old. Jen was disabled but she wasn't stupid. Despite this rude treatment, she would always remain polite, calm and cheerful; even though I know inwardly it hurt her badly.

Diversity is very important to me. I like being around people who are different. They enlighten and inspire me. Ever since Rick Hodges set me straight about my own misconceptions, I have tried to suspend judgment about people until I really get to know them. Prejudice can be very subtle. Please try to maintain an open mind at all times while dealing with others who are different from you. They may be different, but they are not stupid. They deserve all of the respect and dignity that we would afford anyone else, including ourselves.

IN PRAISE OF POCKET PROTECTORS

It wasn't too long ago that I had both the pleasure and pain of watching my youngest daughter, Allison, graduate from high school. It was a pleasure because like most parents I am extremely proud of my two daughters. It was painful for two reasons. First, it marked an unofficial end of our childrearing years. My wife and I would soon join the ranks of "empty nesters." Such milestones are always bittersweet. Mostly it was painful because these graduation ceremonies tend to be very long and at times very boring.

At the risk of sounding cynical, these programs are basically all alike. You can always count on hearing a speech from some faculty member talking about how these kids are our future, how hard they worked, and how confident we can all be in their future success. You can also count on a few top students proclaiming how proud they were to go to this school, how much they learned, and how even though they are now going their separate ways, they will still be friends forever. That is what I expected, and that is what I got. What I didn't expect was Nathan.

Despite his immense popularity, Nathan might be considered - well, a little different. He is extremely smart, not particularly athletic, shy around girls, and through four years of high school could almost always be seen wearing a neatly pressed button down shirt with a pocket protector. As class valedictorian, Nathan was required to address his class and the audience at the commencement ceremony. He received a two-minute standing ovation and several bursts of confetti as he was called to the podium. Rather than blather on with the usual boring clichés, Nathan chose to discuss something very near and dear to his heart...his pocket protector. Why wear a pocket protector? Nathan explained that it is more than just a tool. It is a symbol for how we ought to live. He gave three examples:

1. A pocket protector is designed to shield us from unexpected mishaps, such as exploding pens. This very inexpensive device acts as a protective barrier, costing us little while saving us from greater expenses. We should always be prepared for the unexpected. We should always practice preventive medicine. Whether it is a pocket protector shielding a nice shirt, or a healthy lifestyle that protects us from sickness and disease, it is important to prevent mishaps before they happen.

2. A pocket protector enables us to carry the basic tools required to do our job. In Nathan's pocket you might find two mechanical pencils, two pens and a protractor with a ruler. These basic tools enable him to perform the tasks expected of him as a high school or college student. Shouldn't we all go to work with the right tools to do the job?

3. In his pocket, Nathan carries a spare pencil and a spare pen. Should a fellow student or coworker find they are unprepared for the job at hand (perhaps their pen exploded and ruined their expensive and unprotected shirt), Nathan would be able to assist his teammate by offering one of his. His pocket protector affords him the ability to carry extra tools. Most importantly it allows him to help others. We all work as part of a team. It is very important that we can do our job properly, but it is just as important that we can assist others in achieving a common goal.

Three basic principles. Be prepared for the unexpected. Have the right tools to do the job. Help others. Can anything be more simple? Thank you, Nathan, for a well-taught lesson.

IT'S OKAY TO ASK FOR HELP

It has long been one of the cardinal rules for managers that you should never get involved in the personal lives of the people you supervise. At times this can be difficult. I care very deeply about anyone who has ever worked for me. I may wear the title of manager, but I am still a coworker and a friend. It is hard not to get involved. Just the same, I do agree that there is danger in fraternization. Others may see friendship as favoritism. Likewise, the person you have a beer with today may have to be fired tomorrow. It tends to get messy. There are, of course, exceptions to every rule. As usual there are stories to be told and lessons to be learned.

Sandra worked for me in Manchester, Connecticut. Every day, she took a bus into town from her apartment in East Hartford. Sandy was a terrific employee, had a great work ethic and was loved by all of her coworkers. There was never a problem. When I transferred to East Hartford, I brought Sandra with me. There her performance went into steady decline. One day I called her into my office to discuss her substandard performance. It was then that I learned she had a drug and alcohol problem. Closer to home meant being closer to bad influences. We got her into a rehab program and she did very well for a while. When she had a relapse several months later, I was quick to recognize the warning signs and quick to get her help. She left the company after her second rehab and moved away for a while. A few years later, she stopped by my office to visit. Sandy was doing very well. She made the trip back because she wanted me to know that our helping her the way we did, probably saved her life. That thank-you from Sandy meant more to me than almost any praise or recognition I have ever received.

While at the East Hartford location, I was contacted by a social services organization that tries to help "at risk" students stay out of trouble by finding them jobs. The organization provides a job coach and pays for their first two months in the hope that the employer might want to keep them on once the program is complete. We got Thomas. Tom lived in the toughest part of Hartford's North End. Poverty, crime and violence were nothing new to him. Yet there was something about Tom that made me think he would be okay. I insisted that he bring his schoolwork with him, so we could help with it when he was on break. Tom was a great worker. I hired him after just two weeks. He stayed for two years. A short while ago I ran into him at a local pizza place. He is twenty-four, married, and has a three-year-old son. Tom put himself through tech school and now does electronics repair. He credits his success to the interest we showed in him. We were the role models and mentors that he so desperately needed.

Not every story has a happy ending. Tina had worked for me in Manchester for a few months. She was a good employee but was rumored to have a drinking problem. She was fired for attendance issues. A few years later, while working in East Hartford, I hired her back. I rehired her mostly as a favor to her mother who was a waitress at a nearby diner that I frequented. She got off to a good start, but soon became inconsistent and unreliable. On a Tuesday afternoon, I called her into the office to let her know that her performance needed to improve. It was our last conversation. Two days later she was dead from a heroin overdose.

There are even more tragic examples than Tina. In 1999, I had a wonderful assistant named Mayra. She was bright, energetic and had a promising future. She was a great employee, a great person and a newlywed. We all saw the signs of domestic violence. Carlos was mad at her. She had bruises from "bumping into things." She was afraid of Carlos. We all saw the signs. It was a common topic of gossip. No one did anything. No one said anything. In June 2000, Mayra was murdered. She was strangled to death by Carlos after a particularly heated argument. Mayra was seven months pregnant.

It has always been my belief that managers, executives and supervisors need to be extremely cautious, holding ourselves to the highest of professional standards. That doesn't stop us from caring and taking a personal interest in the well-being of our coworkers. Most companies pride themselves on having an Open Door Policy. While there are limits to involvement, it is important that employees know that the door is always open to discuss problems and concerns. Sometimes we can help. If we cannot, we can usually recommend someone who can. It's okay to ask for help. It's difficult, but okay. Help prevent another tragedy.

One final note. Bosses need help, too. I am neither proud nor ashamed to admit that at various times in my life I have spoken with a therapist, psychiatrist and marriage counselor. I have even sat in on a couple of Alcoholics Anonymous meetings. It's okay to ask for help. Really.

IT MAY BE SOMETHING

It's probably nothing. How often have you heard that? How often have you said it? If it gets worse I'll see about getting it checked out. I don't have time right now. I feel fine. I'm sure it's no big deal. I don't have other symptoms. It's just a cold, a bruise, a wart, a sore. Yes, it is probably nothing, but it may be something. Every year I have both the honor and misfortune of writing and reciting eulogies for fallen friends, coworkers or relatives. In almost every case their demise began as something that was probably nothing.

On Sunday, March 15, 2009, at 11:35 p.m., 57-year-old Diana Baratta passed away at Johnson Memorial Hospital in Somers, Connecticut. She died of complications stemming from both breast and bone cancer. It is a cruel fact of life that people die from cancer all of the time. What makes Diana's case significant? Two things. First, she was one of my wife's closest friends. The two women had been like sisters for more than forty years. Second and more important is the fact that it didn't have to happen. Diana was a victim of "It's probably nothing."

In early January, I ran into Diana at my local pharmacy where she had gone to pick up a prescription for her husband Dan. We talked a bit. She was complaining about a nagging cough that was making her ribs hurt. My wife had just gotten over a hefty case of bronchitis, so I suggested that she may have picked it up from her. She agreed, but mentioned that she hadn't been to see a doctor in several years and most likely would just tough it out. In 19 out of 20 cases it would have been nothing. She was number twenty. Two weeks later I saw her husband Dan at a gas station. He took me aside and we talked. Diana did go to see a doctor. She had been diagnosed with cancer and was given only two months to live. Diana lasted less than six weeks.

Several months earlier, Diana had found a lump on her breast. It was big enough to notice, but not big enough to worry about. She figured she would monitor it, and if it got any larger she could have it checked out. It never grew. Instead, the cancer spread to her bones. It took up residency in her ribs and hip. Meanwhile, the breast cancer led to an infection behind her lungs. It was the infection that killed her.

Diana's story is by no means unusual. Several years ago Bob Carbone, a longtime friend and coworker, was complaining about a pain in his jaw that also was giving him headaches. Weeks passed before the pain grew so bad that he saw a doctor. In Bob's case, what originally started as lung cancer had spread to his brain. He too was 57 when he died.

I am not suggesting that anyone become a hypochondriac. Just because you have a headache does not mean that you have a brain tumor. If you have a headache, take an aspirin. If the headache gets worse or doesn't go away, or you develop additional symptoms, please get it checked out. You may just be buying yourself a little piece of mind. Or you may be saving your own life.

One final thought. The best cure has always been prevention and early detection. The day I learned of Diana's cancer, I called our family doctor and scheduled appointments for both my wife and myself to get complete physicals. A physical is your best bet for early detection. Likewise, a healthy lifestyle is always your best means of prevention. Eat right. Exercise. Get enough sleep. Don't smoke. Practice moderation. If you do encounter a health condition that you know isn't right, get it checked out - immediately. Yeah, it's probably nothing - but can you really afford to take that chance?

LET'S TALK ABOUT THE L-WORD

Probably the most difficult and misunderstood position in any major corporation is that of CEO. We all know that it is the top executive and essentially the captain of the ship, but what does the job actually consist of? In some ways it is very similar to another very high profile position—President of the United States.

First and foremost, you are a figurehead and the face of the organization. Second, you are given the daunting and almost impossible task of keeping a number of conflicting entities, each with its own priorities and agenda, at least somewhat satisfied with the state of affairs. For the President this would be Congress, the American people, foreign nations, the military, etc. The CEO, meanwhile, works for the shareholders, the employees, and the best interest of the company as a whole. In both cases you are on the job 24 hours a day, seven days a week. In both cases an absurd amount of time is spent sitting in meetings.

Meetings certainly are important. There are meetings to plan ahead, to recap old plans, to change plans mid-course, to discuss budgets, or new strategies, or to simply brainstorm. Sometimes there are meetings just to decide where and when the next meeting will be. All meetings, at some level, are intended to be an exchange of information.

A few years ago, I attended a holiday party at a relative's house and found myself chatting with the CEO of a major corporation. He told me the single most important attribute that any top executive can have is to be a good listener. That credo was so important to him that he began every meeting by putting a big letter L in the top right hand corner of his notepad, then circling it. The L is for LISTEN. Throughout any meeting he would glance at the L and remind himself to give complete attention to what was being said. He would then process that information before offering his input.

Most of us, including myself, are not very good listeners. We think we are, but we are not. Often we pretend to be listening, when really we are just waiting for our turn to talk. Other times we daydream, latching on to a single phrase or idea that has been spoken, while missing out on the rest of the discussion. It sounds simple, but listening is an extremely difficult skill to master. It's worth the effort. The best listeners I know are also some of the smartest and most productive people around.

They learn and understand things that get past most of us, just by paying close attention.

It seems to me that there are two important aspects to this skill. The first part is to grasp what is being said. The second is to understand what has been left unsaid. As a manager, if someone tells me that they would like more responsibility, I will understand it to mean that they are willing and able to be more productive than they currently are. What is unsaid may be that they are bored and dissatisfied with their job, or perhaps they really like their job and have aspirations for advancement. Maybe this is a way for them to say that they have some great ideas to share but need a greater sense of empowerment to move forward. All are possibilities, but if you are only hearing, and not listening, you will not be able to tell the difference.

New mothers are probably the best listeners I know. Have you ever been at someone's house when an infant begins to cry? The mother will almost instantly recognize the call. "That's his hungry cry," she might say, or "diaper changing time," or "that's a tired cry." Most of us wouldn't know one cry from another. It's not ESP or even intuition. It is what the mother has learned from careful listening.

When you stop to think about it, we all have a mother's skills when it comes to some aspect of listening. My brother-in-law is a mechanic. He can diagnose almost any engine problem just by listening to it. Your doctor may decide how to treat your cold by listening to various sounds in your cough or your breathing. A talented musician will hear tones that are indiscernible to our ears. We listen when it is important to us, but tend to ignore listening's significance in many of our daily interactions.

I believe the executive I met at that party is indeed correct. Being a good listener is among the most important aspects of a CEO's job. It is also among the most important aspects of almost every other job. If mom's, mechanics, doctors, musicians and CEOs can master the art of listening, then so can we. You will have plenty of opportunities to talk. Be patient. Be quiet. Then listen and think before you speak.

MORE "GOOD OL' DAYS" ARE COMING

It has been my good fortune to have traveled a bit, visiting some of the world's great cities, as well as a few exotic places. Yet for reasons that I cannot adequately explain, Key West and the Florida Keys are by far my favorite vacation locations. They are special places that my wife and I have been to more than a dozen times in the past twenty years. In many ways they are like a second home. The streets, shops and many of the faces have become familiar old friends. We no longer visit the tourist destinations, instead opting for the more secluded places that only the residents know about. For many years I even subscribed to their local newspaper.

Every time I go to Key West it never fails that I have a conversation with someone who is upset about how much the island has changed. They talk about the good old days before the big-money condominiums were built. They recall with misty eyes how the shrimp boats used to tie up to the docks where the cruise ships are now. They talk of the perfume industry and the cigar industry which are now long gone. They complain of bad government selling out the locals to real estate developers. My God, how they miss the good old days.

I go to Key West almost every year. I, too, see changes. Some are good. Some are not so good. At its heart, the island is still the same place that I fell in love with years ago. It is still a haven for writers, artists, musicians and anyone who wants to expatriate without leaving the country. It is still a tiny tourist town that lacks glitter or attitude. There isn't much to do in the Keys that does not involve relaxing. The weather, the water and the people are as warm and inviting as you will find anywhere. Yes, it has changed over the years. Yes, the good old days were great. But it is still great. Changes had to come as a result of hurricanes and various economic and environmental issues. Key West simply did what it had to do to survive in a world that was transforming itself around the island. I still love the place and can't wait to go back.

A couple of months ago I attended a management seminar in Las Vegas. Every time I go to one of these meetings, I never fail to have a conversation with someone who is upset about how much our company has changed over the years. Admittedly, I too have been guilty of looking back with a bit too much fondness. Over the past 20-plus years I have been a part of a company that has grown eight times over in size. Economic, technological and social changes have completely altered the nature of our business. Twenty years ago at a similar seminar, we triumphantly announced that we were ascending to the magical number of seven billion dollars in annual sales. Nowadays that is a very good month. Rapid growth is followed by rapid change. This brings growing pains, followed by more change. Yet a lot doesn't change. At its heart, this is still a company that is trying to be sensitive to the needs of both its customers and its employees, while adapting to a changing world outside. It isn't an easy thing to accomplish, but it is necessary and worthwhile.

I miss the good old days. I miss shrimp boats, Key West Aloe and hand-rolled Cuban seed cigars. I still don't like having cruise ships or luxury condos on my island - but it is my island and I still love it. I know it has to adapt to survive. Every year I look forward to being there, even as these changes are happening.

I also miss the good old days at my company. Yes, it has become so large that some of the feeling of family and community has been lost. But this is my chosen career and my company and I know that it has to adapt and change to survive. I look forward to being there even as these changes continue. Looking forward, I am quite sure that 20 years from now I will look back and fondly remember these days as the good old days, too.

MY KIND OF HERO

It was a bad day in a bad place. On October 25, 2007, a small group of soldiers on patrol in a Taliban stronghold in Afghanistan found themselves ambushed, pinned down and under attack. Surrounded on three sides, the fearless yet undermanned group fought valiantly, sustaining numerous casualties. Each soldier did his job. Each fought heroically. One stood out.

Seizing an opportunity to save a fallen comrade, Staff Sergeant Salvatore Giunta charged directly into enemy fire to rescue one soldier and assist another, both of whom had been shot and captured. Sal was shot four times as he ran into a clearing, firing his weapon and taking down two Taliban soldiers. This enabled him to reach and ultimately bring to safety his fellow platoon members. Thankfully, the protective vest he was wearing successfully stopped the four shots he sustained. Sal escaped without serious injury. One of the two soldiers he rescued survived.

In a White House ceremony on November 16, 2010, President Obama awarded Staff Sergeant Giunta the highest honor that any soldier can receive, the Congressional Medal of Honor. It was the first time in nearly 40 years that the award was bestowed on a living active duty service member. By all accounts, particularly by those who survived the ambush, this shy 25-year-old Iowa native was most deserving, and a true hero in every sense of the word. He put his own fears, concerns, safety and self-interest aside and did whatever he could to assist others in need. I think that is a pretty good definition of a hero.

Salvatore does not want to be a hero and certainly does not think of himself as one. He is bittersweet as he mourns the loss of those who did not survive the battle, thinking - perhaps he could have done more. Sal will tell you he simply did his job that day, as others would have, and as others that day did different but equally important jobs. He did not seek glory, and certainly wished he could have been anywhere else - but he was there, so he did his job.

When television commentator Leslie Stahl interviewed him for a 60-Minutes program, she asked him rather openly, "What kind of soldier are you?" Giunta shook his head modestly and replied, "Mediocre. Average. Nothing special." Ms. Stahl seemed shocked by his response. He then let go of a smile that betrayed the deep pride hidden below. "You should see what the really good ones are like."

Perhaps Salvatore Giunta will cash in on his sudden fame and prominence. I suspect he will not, but I will think no less of him if he does. No doubt Hollywood is clamoring at this very moment for the opportunity to bring his story to life. I'm sure there are book offers, requests for television interviews and maybe even product endorsements. America needs heroes, and this handsome Iowa soldier has quite a story to tell. But Sal Giunta seems to know who he is and who he wants to be. Being a hero is not part of his plan.

It is impossible for me to read or hear of Giunta's story and not feel great pride and admiration for him. He is my kind of hero. He is the kind of person I would hope we all aspire to be. Mr. Giunta is a simple, modest man who wishes to do the best he can regardless of hardship and circumstances. He takes great pride in his coworkers and is more interested in seeing the whole group succeed, rather than accumulate individual praise and recognition. His character is a sure recipe for success in any occupation or business. His actions on that dreadful October day may have made him a hero, but his characteristics every day are what make him heroic.

It was once said of a certain celebrity athlete, that he would gladly give you the shirt off his back if he could first call a press conference to announce he was doing it. That is nothing more than self-promotion. It is not charity and it is not in any way heroic. I want my heroes to teach me something about humility. I want them to deflect their praise by praising others. I want them to do great deeds, and then shrug it off as just another day at the office. I want more people like Sal. America and all Americans are right to praise and honor Staff Sergeant Giunta. Let's hope we can all learn from him as well.

THIS IS NOT JUST ANOTHER "WHEN I WAS IN THE NAVY" STORY...

Okay, maybe it is.

It is unequivocal and undeniable that the short time I spent in the military had a profound influence on the rest of my life. I have often said that I learned more in five minutes in the Navy than I did in four years of college. That is no knock on academia or the value of a good education, but there are some things that you just cannot learn from a textbook.

Everyone talks about teamwork. Nobody teaches teamwork like the military. Every person begins his or her tour of duty with a six to twelve week indoctrination called Basic Training or Boot Camp. For me this was eight weeks in Great Lakes, Illinois, just north of Chicago on the shores of Lake Michigan. During that time, recruits are slowly and sometimes painfully transformed from clinging to the idea of "me" to grasping the importance of "we."

Our unit was Troop 359. We called ourselves Goodman's Glory, out of respect for our Company Commander, Electrician's Mate First Class Charles M. Goodman. For many, the toughest part of the eight weeks was the physical training. We marched, we ran, we did pushups, sit ups, squats, and an incredibly painful drill called "butterfly kicks." We were timed and tested. During the final week of training there were tests for everything.

I know it may be hard to imagine now, but I really was in very good physical shape back then. I knew basic training would be hard so I worked out and ran extensively prior to taking active duty. I could do 50 pushups without missing a beat, and run a mile in six minutes flat. Not everyone took it so seriously. Let's be honest — we had some fat guys.

A week before our final exam we were told that for the running test we had to do two miles in eighteen minutes. No problem. I could do that without breaking a sweat. The fat guys were in trouble. Then they told us that we were being graded as a unit. Either everyone passes or everyone fails. That's how it works in combat. If someone doesn't do his part, everyone gets killed.

Their reasoning was sound, but what could we do about the four guys who didn't stand a chance? Six of us secretly met late one night to discuss the problem. First, we thought about roughing them up so they would be too injured to participate. We actually liked these guys so that was quickly ruled out. Other options were considered. After a while a real solution came to us. The six fastest runners, me included, would stay in the back of the group. When the running drill began we would lock arms with the four heavyweights and run with them. Really, we dragged them most of the way, but their feet were moving so it looked like they were running. They did their best to keep up as we pulled them along. It worked. We crossed the finish line with just ten seconds to spare.

The six of us could have easily finished the race first, but instead 10 of us finished last. In doing so we learned a valuable lesson that none of us would ever forget. A team is not made up of a bunch of individuals. It is a single united group.

How many times in our jobs or our lives are we faced with a situation where, if one person fails, everyone fails? Think about it and you will realize that it happens quite regularly. How many times did you carry someone across the finish line? How many times were you carried? We're all in this together.

OCCAM AND KISS

It is a minor coincidence, but recently, while on vacation, I read two novels. Both made reference to something called "Occam's Razor." In the context of what I was reading there was a sense of what this meant, but I wanted to know more. I soon found myself Googling the term to get a complete definition. It turns out that William of Occam was a medieval philosopher and scientist. Occam's Razor is defined as the belief that "entities must not be multiplied beyond necessity." This idea has since been rewritten in many other ways, and is now more commonly quoted as, "When given a problem, choose the simplest solution until it proves to be incorrect or ineffective." Most of us have never heard of Occam or his razor, but we have heard of KISS. Keep it simple, stupid. It's the same thing.

Keep it simple. This is easier said than done. We live in a complicated, high tech, fast paced world where nothing seems easy. Our lives are constantly being directed by technology, legalities and political correctness. In many ways we have become comfortable with this burden. If something isn't detailed or difficult, there must be something wrong with it.

This need to complicate things is everywhere, including in our personal lives. Think about the last time you and a group of others decided to go out to dinner at a restaurant. Perhaps you quickly agreed on Italian food. Then what happened? The indecisive questions take over. What kind of Italian? Pizza, pasta or seafood? How far do you want to drive? How much do you want to spend? By the time you finally reach a decision, the restaurant is probably closed. Some would say the problem is that we have too many choices. Occam would say that we are not keeping it simple. When faced with such a decision, why not go with the nearest restaurant that you know you like? Once there you will undoubtedly find a menu item to match your taste.

Most businesses could use a healthy dose of Occam and KISS. As a manager, I share much of the blame for making things more complicated than they need to be. We often have meetings, conferences, emails and memos. As a result, we have a never-ending stream of programs, directives and initiatives. Meetings and conferences can be good. They give us increased communication. Directives are good. They provide us with instruction and guidelines. Making things overly complicated is not good.

Businesses constantly talk about customer service issues. There are tons of programs and guidelines for this. Why not keep it simple? Treat every customer and every customer service situation by asking yourself, "If I was that person, how would I want to be treated?"

Businesses constantly talk about sales. The easiest way to create sales is to have what your customers want, when they want it, delivered in a convenient and affordable manner. Most companies spend a fortune on marketing, but the best marketing tool is to sell a good product at a good price.

Businesses constantly talk about expense control. If you spent every dollar as though it were coming out of your own pocket, you would spend less. You don't need another program or initiative to tell you that. If you question each purchase by asking if it is really a necessity, you will have the best expense control possible.

Businesses have employee relations departments that are set up with one purpose in mind — to ensure that their employees are treated fairly. Occam would have a hard time understanding why this exists. Treat your employees as you would like to be treated. Keep it simple.

While not every question or problem can be solved with a short, singular response, many can. Look for the basic, logical approach first before moving on to more complicated solutions. Even the most difficult problems are best addressed when we break them down into a series of smaller, more easily managed tasks. KISS. Keep it simple. There is nothing stupid about that.

ONE DAY AT A TIME

I have known Daniel as a friend and neighbor for the past few years. He is a husband, a father, an engineer and an alcoholic. Dan hit bottom three years ago after his second drunk driving arrest. As was mandated by the court system, he began attending Alcoholics Anonymous. Most weeks he will go to three meetings. While AA meetings are supposed to be confidential, Dan has no problem talking about them with his friends.

The story Dan tells that sticks with me most is the one about meeting his sponsor. All regular AA members pick a sponsor to help them with their recovery. It was somewhat ironic that Daniel, a rather polished white collar professional, would choose Jack as his mentor. Jack is a large, burly and gruff truck-driver from a neighboring town. While they didn't have much in common besides alcohol addiction, for some reason they seemed to hit it off. Jack is often bold and intimidating. Mild-mannered Dan figured that he was the kind of person he would need to help him stay sober.

During their first meeting together, Jack told Dan that he had just one question for him. That question was, "Would you go to any length to stay sober? Specifically, would you leave your wife and kids for a year, move out of state, maybe out of the country, and work for a charity for a year, if that was what it would take to keep you sober?" Jack then told him to think about it and he would see him tomorrow to get his answer.

Dan didn't sleep at all that night. He knew his life was a mess and he needed to stay sober, but this was a bit extreme. Still, he didn't want to blow his chances for recovery by not going along with the program. He tossed and turned all night as he pondered the question. Finally, when he and Jack met, he told him quite honestly, "No. As much as I want to conquer my demons, that is asking too much." Jack smiled. "I agree. I wouldn't do it either. On the other hand, do you think you could do it for a day?" Dan suddenly felt his burden lifted. Sure he could. He could do almost anything for a day. "That's all we are asking," Jack replied. "Do whatever it takes not to drink today. When tomorrow comes, start over and do whatever it takes not to drink on that day as well. The road to success is paved one day at a time."

Dan's story rings true with me on many levels. It is true for anyone pursuing a career or building a business. It is true in saving money for your own financial security. It is also true in how you deal with adversity, grief, and personal demons. Seize the day. Conquer the day. Somehow make it through the day. Start small and build big.

One day at a time. Big plans need small steps. Never lose sight of your goals, but realize that things take time. Most large companies have an assortment of five-and ten-year plans. It is necessary, because large undertakings require planning, budgeting, materials acquisition, manpower analysis and oversight. Those things take time. While they may not happen instantly, goals are achieved by a series of smaller incremental steps. Day-to-day accomplishments ultimately lead to the desired outcome. It has been said that success comes from doing the little things right, then doing them over and over again. Do what you have to do today. Plan for tomorrow, but today is what will get you there.

One day at a time. That is how a career and a company are built. It is how you overcome adversity. It is how you conquer your demons. It is how you get past personal tragedy. It is how you celebrate victories, both large and small. It is how you achieve your goals and ambitions. You don't have to do it all at once. You can't. Take it one step at a time and one day at a time. You'll get there.

PERCEPTION AS DECEPTION

There is a June 2010 edition of Entertainment Weekly Magazine that has a short piece by writer David Karger in which he discusses an interview he did in 2008 with Angelina Jolie. The interview, which was conducted at a hotel in France, was pleasant, polite and professional. Ms. Jolie was both honest and gracious. As the two left the hotel lobby, they were predictably greeted by the clicking of paparazzi cameras. After walking Ms. Jolie to her car, Mr. Karger extended his hand to thank her for the interview. Ms. Jolie, in keeping with the customs and culture of France, responded with a kiss on the cheek. Within minutes the gossip machine was churning out stories of the actress's infidelities as she emerged from the posh hotel with her handsome new lover. One photographer managed to capture the kiss on the cheek in such a way that an innocent peck looked like a passionate lip lock. The unsuspecting reporter was now the story.

Reality is not always what we know or think we know. Our senses may misguide us. Too little information may lead us to think that we know more than we do. Too much information may cause us to draw an incorrect conclusion. In some cases, a good person who is behaving in an appropriate manner may appear to be quite the scoundrel. This can have a damaging effect on someone both professionally and personally. Perception may be deception. This is especially true for those in the public eye, but it also applies to those who hold leadership roles in the business world. Our actions and our intentions are often misinterpreted by others.

Some years ago, I had an outstanding young manager, Edward, working for me. He was dedicated, personable and had a tireless work ethic. Above all, Ed was and still is a genuinely good person. Early one evening, Ed was walking past the break room when he noticed that an employee was sitting at the table, head in her hands, sobbing. This employee had recently lost her husband and was having a hard time adjusting. Edward sat with her a while, consoling and comforting as best he could. Once she regained her composure, the employee gave him a gentle hug, thanking him for being so understanding. The following morning another employee stopped by my office to speak to me.

She couldn't wait to report that my top assistant and a coworker were "making out" in the break room last night.

On another occasion I had an employee ask if she could speak to me privately for a moment. I readily obliged, and asked that others take my calls, so we would not be interrupted. We then went into my office for a brief, closed door discussion. The employee wished to apologize for several recent absences, explaining that she was having some health issues related to menopause. She was embarrassed and didn't want this to be public knowledge, but she also felt that I deserved an honest explanation for her sick calls. I thanked her for speaking to me and asked if she needed any help with regards to our company's medical benefits. A few minutes later an assistant saw me and asked if I had fired her. A bit confused, I asked him where he got that idea from. He replied that he knows she's been unreliable so when I called her into the office and closed the door he assumed I was letting her go.

Once, not too long ago, I was speaking by phone with my boss, discussing a local competitor that was going out of business. The conversation was primarily about how we might best attract their customers and whether or not we would want to interview and possibly hire a few of their employees. Most of the discussion took place on my cell phone within earshot of a number of coworkers. Later that day two very concerned employees came to me and asked if we were going out of business. They had overheard me talking about liquidating and layoffs and were now fearful for their jobs.

In each of these cases a little information caused a lot of confusion. What can be done about misinformation? Should we have an environment where we need to be afraid to show compassion or offer a coworker a few private moments of our time? Do we need to mute every word we say, allowing no one else to ever hear part of a conversation? I certainly hope not. We do, however, need to be aware of our own words and actions so that when confronted with misinformation we are prepared to address the issue. We also need to foster an environment where open dialogue is encouraged and gossip is shunned. That will keep the conversations flowing and the paparazzi away.

PLAYING HURT

As a kid growing up in the late 1960s and early 1970s, I had two sports heroes. One was Johnny Unitas and the other was Thurman Munson. These two athletes were probably the two toughest individuals that I have ever seen on a field of competition.

For 17 years, Johnny Unitas was the legendary quarterback for the Baltimore Colts. An often told story is how during one game he took a particularly hard hit from an opposing linebacker. The end result of that play was a broken nose. Before the team's medical personnel could get to him, and before his coach could pull him from the game, Unitas reached down and pulled a handful of sod from the field. He then jammed the turf into his nostrils to stop the bleeding, and quickly returned to the huddle. On the next play he threw a touchdown pass. I really don't know if the story is true, but few who ever saw Johnny play would doubt that it could be.

A similar story that I know is true because I saw it happen, involves former New York Yankees catcher Thurman Munson. In the third inning of the first game of a double header, there was a close play at home plate. When the long throw came in from the outfield, the ball took an errant bounce and hit Thurman squarely in the mouth. His lip was cut and a couple of teeth were either chipped or knocked loose. His manager and the team trainer rushed out to help their star player from the field. Munson refused to go. While repeatedly spitting blood, he argued for several minutes with his manager until finally the home plate umpire intervened and ordered him from the field. He was taken to a nearby hospital where he received several stitches and numerous shots of Novocain. Once released from the hospital, he took a cab back to the ballpark. By the third inning of the second game he was back behind home plate.

It is very unlikely that either of these two incidents could happen today, and in a way that's a shame. In our current time, when athletes earn tens of millions of dollars each year, teams have become extremely cautious with their players, benching them for the most minor of injuries. The belief is that a short absence is better than risking a longer one. I understand their reasoning, but I don't like it. I admire people who can work through pain.

In the workplace we see both sides of this spectrum. There are those who will show up to work from their deathbed, spreading disease and germs to all who come near. Broken bones, surgeries, flu and pneumonia are minor inconveniences. They reason that if they have to be sick and miserable, they might as well get paid for it. Time off from work is to enjoy a good day, not lie at home in bed.

Then there are the hangnail sissies. These are people who call out sick a day ahead of time because they think they may be getting a cold, or because they have a small splinter that needs immediate medical attention. They can't come to work because it will only make them feel worse. Besides, the company gives them sick days, so why not use them? They have little regard for the inconveniences that their absence will create.

As with most things in life there needs to be a balance. If you are contagious and may be responsible for infecting numerous others, then you have a duty to seek immediate medical care, and return to work when you are no longer a threat to others. If you are hurt and cannot possibly perform your expected duties to even a marginal degree, then by all means you should stay home and mend. On the other hand, not every minor malady is cause enough to visit a doctor or stay home in bed. Sometimes you just have to tough it out.

I am more inclined to favor those who play through pain. When you are younger there is a tendency to get so caught up in the moment that you ignore bumps and bruises. As you grow older, you come to accept aches and pains as an everyday part of life. In each case you need to be aware that other people are counting on you. If it is reasonably possible, then you should be there. The way I see it, if you can function at a level that is at least fifty percent of your full capacity, it is still better than having others trying to cover for you while at the same time performing their own jobs. Only you know what your capacity is.

Unitas and Munson were two of the toughest guys to ever set foot on a field of sport. No one is expected to play through pain the way they did. Likewise, no one is expected to be an ironman like Orioles shortstop Cal Ripken Jr. who for 17 years never missed a day of work. All that is expected is for you to be reliable. Very reliable. And sometimes that may mean playing hurt.

PUT ON A HAPPY FACE

Acting is one of the most important yet least talked about manage-ment skills there is. Since the term itself implies pretending, it is impor-tant to distinguish good acting from false pretense or phony, insincere gestures. Most companies are filled with yes-men and butt-kissers who coddle up to their corporate superiors in hopes of gaining favor. That is not acting and it is not at all productive. What I mean by acting is the ability to display a positive attitude, even in tough times, and particularly during times when a frown and a scowl would be your natural and pre-ferred demeanor.

Let's assume I had a bad morning. Maybe I had a spat with my wife, or the dog got into the trash, or I spilled hot coffee on myself. By the time I get to work I already hate everything and everybody. That's my problem, not everybody else's. Before stepping from my car I have an obligation to compose myself, leave those earlier issues behind me, and put on a big confident smile. If I don't, the rest of the day will surely get worse. If I fail to pull myself together and pretend to be my usually upbeat self, my bad mood will surely become contagious. The bad attitude is immediately noticed. Everyone gets nervous. There is a murmur of unrest. Talk starts. What's wrong with the boss? Did I do something wrong? Did you hear how he snapped at that vendor? Before long, nobody is productive and everyone is unhappy, all because of a bad mood that started with some-thing completely unrelated to work.

Another example: Perhaps things have fallen behind. There is more work to be done than you could ever hope to accomplish. You are in danger of missing deadlines, and corporate leadership is breathing down your back. Two people quit on short notice. Computer problems are abounding. The air conditioner isn't working, the roof is leaking, and there is a strange odor coming from the lavatory. As they say — when it rains it pours. It's pouring.

Once again you find yourself in the parking lot, with your head pressed against the steering wheel thinking this is the last place in the world you want to be. What do you do? Once again you take a deep breath and put on that big confident smile. As you walk through the doors, cowork-ers bombard you with a thousand questions and a look of panic. No problem. You boldly assure them that all is well. You have a plan. Sure there are challenges, but we can all work to resolve them. Everything is going to be okay. The truth is that you may have no clue, but if everyone believes things are going to be fine, the chances are greatly increased that they will be. Soon coworkers rally to the cause. They volunteer extra hours, extra help, and great ideas. A real plan of action soon develops and problems get resolved. On the other hand, just imagine what would happen if you walked in with the look of fear and panic on your face. A bad situation would quickly get much worse.

Admittedly, in both of these scenarios it may be easier said than done. In that case honesty is your best first and last resort. What should you do if you are in a foul mood that you just can't shake? When you get to work, tell everyone. You don't have to be specific. Just let them know that you are having a rough day and apologize if you don't seem to be yourself right now. At least give them the assurance that they have done nothing wrong. The same goes for being overwhelmed. Gather your key personnel. Articulate to them the daunting challenges that you are facing. Tell them frankly and honestly that you do not have all of the answers and really need their help. If you have been fair and supportive of your employees, it is a safe bet that they will rally to support you.

Maybe it's acting. Maybe it's even a little bit phony. Or maybe it's just a matter of turning a bad situation into a good one by using the right attitude. The happy-face approach applies well to management, but it is no less applicable to any job, relationship or obstacle. Optimism is contagious. So are fear, panic and despair. What worries you outside of work? Money? Family? Health issues? First, resolve to yourself that it is not the end of the world and that no matter what, things will get better. Convince yourself of this, even if it seems like false hope. Then set to work on a plan. I don't know of any great challenge that was ever overcome without optimism, enthusiasm and a little bit of acting. Trust me, it works.

SLEEPING THROUGH STORMS

I really don't know why, but every year as January comes around, I find myself making three or four New Year's resolutions. Over the years I must have made hundreds of them. Lose weight, exercise more, eat right, worry less, watch less television, read more, write more, take a class, pay off bills, have more patience, give more to charity, don't swear, be a better husband, father, friend and person. All were made with good intentions. Some I managed to keep, but most were broken by January 2nd. One that I have kept and will continue to strive to keep is to sleep through storms.

One of my favorite writers, Mitch Albom, likes to talk about the sermons that his former rabbi used to give. In one particular sermon, the rabbi tells the story of a local farmer who was interviewing for a new lead farmhand. After speaking with a number of prospective candidates, he had settled on one in particular. As a final step in the process, the farmer asked the young man if he had any references or letters of recommendation. "Just one" was the reply as he handed over a single sheet of paper. It was from the young man's last employer, and it simply read "He sleeps through storms." Despite being a bit confused over the letter, the farmer hired the man. For the next two years the two worked very well together.

One night while watching the eleven o'clock news, the farmer saw that a terrible storm was heading their way. He immediately sprang from his chair and raced to the farmhand's quarters. Pounding on the door he shouted, "Get up! Big storm coming! Lots to do. We have to get ready quick!" The farmer pounded and pounded, shouted and shouted, but the young man did not stir. The farmer knew he was in there. He could hear him snoring. Angry and frustrated, the farmer raced to the barn. There he found that all the hay they had cut down earlier in the day was neatly baled, bound and stacked. Checking his livestock, he soon realized that the animals were all safe, locked in their pens or paddocks with extra bedding, feed and water. Out in the garage, the tractors and plows were all safe and secure, with a full tank of gas, ready for the next time they would be used. It was then that the farmer recalled the letter of reference. It was then that he smiled and quietly went to bed where he, too, slept through the storm.

It is a difficult lesson to learn, but we all need to master the art of sleeping through storms. For sure, storms will come. There will be unexpected setbacks, circumstances and twists of fate. If we work honestly and diligently through the day, preparing for whatever challenges these difficult times may bring, then we, too, can sleep through storms. If we build a solid team, based on trust and cooperation, then we can sleep through storms. If we can go to bed at night knowing that we worked hard and gave the best possible effort to whatever tasks and endeavors that we undertook, then we, too, can sleep through storms. It is one resolution that I have learned to keep. Perhaps it is one that you, too, should make.

SOMETIMES THE BEST THING YOU CAN DO IS JUST WALK AWAY

It's sad to say, but sometimes the most ignorant people you meet are the ones who should otherwise be the most open-minded. Two stories...

On a cold December night a few years ago I attended a women's basketball game between two small New England colleges. My daughter Emily is a student at one of the schools, majoring in business. She also plays on its basketball team. The campus has about a thousand undergrads so a typical game crowd is roughly a hundred fans, consisting mostly of family and students. It doesn't take long before the parents begin to get to know one another.

On this particular night, I sat next to a woman whose daughter was a freshman. We talked throughout the first half of the game about the school and the team. In the course of our conversation, she mentioned that her daughter's second choice was one of Connecticut's state universities. The school that this woman mentioned happens to be where my younger daughter Allison attends as an art major. The woman praised the school as being a beautiful campus with an excellent faculty. She then leaned over and told me that she is glad her daughter isn't going there. She wouldn't feel comfortable since there were so many black students. I was dumbfounded. It was beyond belief to me that an intelligent and articulate person would make such a statement. I had never met this person before. What if I had family members who are black? What if I was actually a light-skinned biracial? I didn't know what to say so I excused myself to use the restroom. When I returned I sat elsewhere in the stands.

A few days later, I received a phone call from a fellow manager and a former assistant regarding a situation involving a problem customer. This particular customer wanted us to perform a service which would have amounted to a copyright infringement. Amy handled the situation with all of the courtesy, tact and skill that she could muster. It wasn't enough. The customer became belligerent and irate. Before long, he was swearing at her, ranting and raving about how horrible it was that she was treating a war veteran this way. Amy, desperate to establish some common ground with this individual, then commented that she, too, was a veteran, having recently served with the Marines in Iraq. The customer became further enraged, saying that she was a liar. She was clearly too young for military service. Prior to slamming the phone down, he asked for and received the number of Amy's supervisor.

When Amy called me, she was understandably upset. I offered what little advice I could, suggesting that she quickly call her boss and inform him of the situation. This way, he wouldn't be blindsided by the imminent irate phone call. She did, and Jim, her supervisor, did the best he could to defuse the problem without violating any copyright laws.

Amy was particularly upset by the fact that this person used his military service as an excuse for inexcusable behavior. I was, too. Both Amy and I are veterans. All of the vets we know are proud of their service, but ask for nothing special or preferential in return.

Both of these situations are disturbing to me. In each case I have repeatedly asked myself if we should have acted differently. What could we have done to show these two people the error of their ways? Sadly, I don't think there is much that could have been done to improve the situation. It is impossible in a two-minute conversation to enlighten an ignorant person. The one thing you should never do in these cases is to validate the person's view. A seemingly harmless comment like "I understand" or "I know what you mean" is in fact a subtle way of saying you agree with them. It is better to say nothing or to try and change the subject.

Ignorance comes in many forms. One person may be a highly educated professional. Another may be a decorated war hero. Both exhibited shameful examples of narrow-mindedness. Although you may be offended and you may want to speak out, sometimes the best you can do is quietly walk away. If you can't stop ignorance, at least don't spread it.

THE FISH GET TO DECIDE

Lower Bolton Lake is a 175-acre expanse of water, nestled in Eastern Connecticut between the towns of Bolton and Coventry. It is home to at least eight species of freshwater fish, but is best known for being stocked annually with a large supply of catfish. A few weeks ago, I was on the lake in my kayak, attempting to catch as many cats as possible. As luck would have it, I had a very successful day. In a relatively short period of time, I caught three "keeper size" largemouth bass and an assortment of other species. No catfish. Bass wasn't what I was fishing for, but I was pleased just the same. Last week I again fished the lake. Same place, same time, same weather, same bait, same techniques. This time I caught four catfish and no bass. A few days ago I returned once more. Again, location and conditions were the same. This time I was catching a seemingly endless supply of yellow perch.

How is it possible that everything seemed the same, yet each time my catch was different? Two reasons. First, although things may have appeared the same, in truth, they were not. Many other factors come into play. The water temperature may have been different. A change in the phases of the moon. A shift in underwater vegetation. The natural movement of fish from one feeding area to another. All of these factors influence what species might be feeding at a given moment. The second reason for my varied catch is a bit more obvious. While I may have done everything correctly in my pursuit of catfish, bass or perch, it is ultimately the fish who get to decide when and if to take the bait. I can entice them with worms, minnows or lures, but if they don't want to take the hook, I can't make them.

Business, sales, and marketing is a lot like fishing. Based on past experiences and the information you have accumulated over time, you do your best to lure new customers. You repeat the techniques that have worked before. You entice prospective customers with great service, competitive pricing and varied product selection. That is the bait. The hope is that they will take the bait and reward you with sales and profits. Very often it works. Sometimes it doesn't. You can do everything right. You can duplicate any past success, but there still are no guarantees.

The customers and clients are the fish who gets to decide. When they choose not to bite, we are left with only one choice. Do something else.

Try something. Try anything. Keep trying until something works. While current conditions might seem familiar, the truth is that they are not. Sales patterns change. Competition changes. Demographics change. The overall economic climate changes. The techniques that it takes to entice and lure customers is always changing. In good times it seems like any bait will work. In hard times we may feel as though nothing works. The key is to keep trying and keep changing. When you do get it right it is important to realize that your success is only temporary.

It is easy to become discouraged and frustrated when the methods of past success no longer yield results. Adaptability is the key. You may need to tweak or you may need to overhaul. Sometimes the best idea is an old one. What did you do differently 10 or 20 years ago? Might that "old way" work today? There is absolutely nothing wrong with revisiting an old idea, or combining it with a new one.

It's all about catching the fish. When they aren't biting you must adjust. Sometimes you change the bait. Sometimes you change the hook. Other times you start from scratch. It is the fish who get to decide, but it is your job to make sure that they choose you.

THE THIRD MAN

Here is a little ghost story with a lesson worth remembering.

Many years ago, an old friend of mine worked as a mate on a shrimp boat. Back in the late 1940s and early 1950s, the Gulf of Mexico was speckled with dozens of these two or three-man enterprises. The work was hard, dirty and dangerous. Bert, the captain, manned the wheel and controlled the hauling winches. As his mate, Tony's duties included cleaning the boat, working the nets and tending to the catch. The pair seldom worked on Sundays, but on one occasion they found themselves trying to avoid a storm, which kept them out at sea for a few days longer than expected. When Bert and Tony sat down to eat their Sunday dinner, Bert insisted that an extra setting be placed on the table. He explained to Tony that on Sunday you should always set a place for the Third Man. Bert believed it was important to pay homage to all of those who had lost their lives at sea. They are the Third Man. They keep us safe.

Several weeks later, Tony and Bert were working the catch on a particularly rough and stormy night. Bert struggled to keep the boat on course, while Tony emptied and sorted the nets. The salt air and rain stung as a very tired mate worked in the cold darkness, under the glow of a single light bulb. As the boat pitched back and forth, the young man struggled to keep his footing. One misstep and he could easily have wound up overboard. Despite crashing waves, Tony somehow managed to hold his place, sorting and emptying hundreds of pounds of shrimp into the vessel's cargo hold.

Suddenly, after one particularly hard roll, he was tossed from his feet and slid sprawling across the deck. It was then that he came face to face with a pale and crusty old sailor in full rain gear staring down at him. Tony scrambled to his feet and ran back to the nets. When he turned to look again, the sailor was gone. The following day, as the storm subsided and the boat returned safely to port, Tony told Bert that he would no longer be working with him. He stammered through a number of excuses, none of which were very convincing. Bert looked him square in the eye and asked, "Was he wearing a yellow slicker?" Tony nodded. "It was the Third Man," Bert replied. "That was a heck of a storm. You could have easily died out there. The Third Man kept you safe."

I don't know if the Third Man story is true or not. Tony was always good for a tall tale. Over the years, I have come to view the Third Man story as a symbolic lesson on the importance of remembering those who came before you. When a sailor is taken by the sea, it is almost always because he made a costly mistake and paid the ultimate price. To pay homage to the Third Man is to learn from the past and use those lessons to build a better future. Past mistakes make us smarter and enable us to be safer, stronger and more prosperous as we move forward. It is an often used and over-quoted saying that those who will not learn from the mistakes of the past are destined to repeat them.

Yet the lessons of the Third Man go far beyond the mistakes of the past. It is important as we move forward in our jobs and in our personal lives, to look back with honor and respect toward those who came before us. They made us what we are today. Their toil, their successes, and, yes, even their mistakes have paved the road to our future. It is great to roll forward with pride, purpose and optimism, but we should always remember to keep a place for the Third Man who keeps us safe.

THEY WORK FOR US

It is almost always an unpleasant experience, but lately I have had the misfortune of having to fire a couple of people. In both cases they were long term-employees of mine. One worked for me for 20 years, the other 10. Luckily, neither of these terminations occurred at my place of employment. No, the two employees I speak of were my insurance agent and my family doctor.

Jake had been my insurance agent for the past 10 years. He would routinely check and update my policy to ensure that I was getting the best rates possible. Whenever I had a question or problem, I would call him, knowing there would be a prompt and knowledgeable response. Somewhere along the way, Jake got lazy. Two years ago, a large maple tree in my yard was killed by a lightning strike. Since then, whenever a storm would pass through with high winds, several large branches would come crashing to the ground. I began to fear that someone or perhaps the house might get hit, causing damage or injury. I called Jake believing that my insurance should cover the cost of the tree removal. It took a while for Jake to return my call. Too long. When he did, he quickly dismissed my request, saying that my policy will cover any damage done, but not the cost of prevention. Something didn't sound right about that, so after six or seven phone calls to the home office, I finally reached a helpful person who agreed with me. I soon received a check and the tree came down.

The tree experience made me begin to question the quality of service that I was getting from Jake. I began talking with other companies and agents who compared policies and prices for me. It turned out that I was overpaying for poor service. I fired Jake as my agent and am now quite pleased with my current insurance provider.

Doc Jones has been our family physician for more than 20 years. Over the past two decades, he has gotten us through everything from broken bones to sinus infections. Initially his knowledge and dedication were outstanding, but over time he, too, got lazy. Four years ago I began to have some doubts about the good doctor. He had misdiagnosed me, mistaking an infection for a more serious condition that would have required immediate surgery. Luckily, another doctor corrected his mistake before I landed on the operating table. Last week, I made an appointment with

Doc Jones for what seemed to be an ear infection. He asked a few questions and checked my ear, but could find nothing wrong. Doctor Jones then concluded that it must be either seasonal allergies or tinnitus. Call him in two weeks if the symptoms didn't improve. Meanwhile, a pharmacist friend had suggested that I might want to try pseudoephedrine and ibuprofen to help relieve the discomfort. When I mentioned this to the doc, he said he hadn't thought of it but quickly agreed. I began to wonder why I was paying him when my pharmacist was addressing the problem he should have handled. Since then I have decided that it is best if we part company. I am firing Doctor Jones.

We don't usually think of it this way, but doctors, insurance agents, lawyers, therapists, accountants, dry cleaners, mechanics, repairmen and countless others all work for us. We employ them to provide goods and services. When they meet or exceed our expectations, we reward them with additional business and word of mouth referrals. When they fail to fulfill our needs, then it is our right to fire them and take our dollars elsewhere.

As you might guess, this works both ways. While our paychecks may come from our employers, we are really employed by our customers. They are the ones who pay us to provide goods and services. They are whom we work for. Usually we meet their expectations. Sometimes we fail. Because of our failings we are fired many times each year, often without ever realizing it. This takes money away from us, our coworkers and our shareholders. It's not hard to find a new insurance agent or doctor and it's not hard for our own patrons to replace us. Simply put, our job is to ensure that more customers hire us than fire us. If we do, we will probably succeed. If we don't we will definitely fail. This is our job and we can't afford to get lazy.

WE ARE ALWAYS ON STAGE

This is an amusing story I heard recently. I assume it is true.

It was one of those unfortunate circumstances. A plane gets stuck for several hours on the tarmac, unable to take off. From the comfort of her seat in the first-class cabin, Dolly Parton was resting, or reading, or listening to music, or counting her money, or doing whatever it is that country music superstars do when they are stuck on a plane. Behind her, in the coach cabin, ordinary travelers were growing uncomfortable and very restless. Reluctantly, a rather nervous flight attendant approached Ms. Parton and asked if she would be kind enough to poke her head into the back cabin and perhaps say a few words to the passengers. It might help them keep the now agitated crowd occupied while they fixed whatever it was that had delayed the flight. Dolly smiled and said that she would be delighted.

For the next hour or two, Dolly Parton sang songs, told stories, signed autographs, took pictures, and completely enthralled her captive audience. By some accounts there were passengers who were actually disappointed when it was announced that the plane would soon be ready for departure. Upon returning to her seat, a fellow first-class passenger leaned over and asked her if she finds it tiring or annoying to always be on stage, even when she is not on stage. Dolly seemed almost insulted by the question. She explained that she has worked extremely hard to become a successful entertainer. Now that she actually is one, the last thing she intends to do is complain about it.

In a world filled with celebrity meltdowns and ambush paparazzi, it is nice to know that Dolly Parton understands her role. Along with the benefits that go with celebrity, or success at any level, comes additional responsibility. Sometimes achieving a high level of success means that you have to work harder and do more than the average person. For Dolly Parton that meant taking a potentially explosive situation and turning it into a joyous one.

Two points of note: By being successful you are expected to do more. There are rewards, but there is a price. That price is more work and greater results. It doesn't matter if you are a singer, an athlete, a manager, mechanic or a clerical worker; if you are very good at what you do, you are always expected to perform at the highest level. Furthermore, because you have the capacity to do more, it is assumed that you should be willing and able to take on additional responsibilities. For an athlete or entertainer that may mean signing autographs or taking part in charity events. For a manager it could mean working extra long hours or becoming involved in local business organizations. For a mechanic or clerical assistant, it may mean training coworkers. That is the price of success.

The other point worth making is that all of us, not just entertainers, are always on stage. We may be at home or at the mall or visiting with friends and family, but we still represent both ourselves and our company. What we do for a living is part of who we are. On some level, others will associate us with our jobs. People see us at work, then pass us again in the grocery store. How you are perceived at work will impact how you are viewed in the outside world. Likewise, how you act when you are out in the community will be considered a reflection on both you as an employee and on your company as a whole.

I have never been a big Dolly Parton fan, but after hearing that story, I am one now. How many fans will you make today? How big is your stage? How good will your performance be? It's not acting. It's just part of the job.

WHAT BASEBALL HAS TAUGHT ME

There is a popular tee shirt found in numerous sportswear shops that proclaims "Baseball is life. Everything else is just details." In fairness, you can also find the same shirt with regards to football, basketball, golf, tennis, dancing and almost any other pastime. I have been a fan of baseball for pretty much my entire life. It is a simple game. Catch, hit, run, and throw. It is a team sport where the individual stands out. It has no clock. Its history and traditions carry meaning. It is marked by dates, statistics and monumental achievements. The game unites friends and divides foes. Baseball is a connecting link from one generation to another. As a young boy, my father instilled in me a passion for the game, and I in turn have passed it on to my daughters.

Baseball has taught me a lot. Many of its lessons have served me quite well in business. Many more have served me well in life. Here are just a few thoughts on some things baseball has taught me:

You can't hit the ball when the bat is on your shoulder. One of the most embarrassing plays in baseball is when a batter strikes out without swinging. We are all faced with opportunities. Many will pass us by as we watch in indecision. Don't be a spectator. Take your chances, even if it means you go down swinging. Be an active part of the situation. Go after what you want.

Keep your head in the game. There are going to be setbacks. If you make an error, or if you are the victim of a bad call, or if you fail at a crucial moment and lose a game, accept it and move on. To dwell too long on what has already happened is to lose focus on what may happen next.

It's a long season. Preparation and conditioning are extremely important. Many games are won and lost before the teams step on the field. Prepare for each day. Stay healthy. Know your opponent. Pace yourself. A quick start does not ensure a strong finish. Make sure you have enough in the tank to see things all the way through.

The best team will usually beat the team with the best players. Team chemistry is important. Surround yourself with positive people who share your goals and whom you enjoy being around. These are the kind of people who will mesh together well and work as one. Nine individuals on the field may be an impressive display of talent but talent will only get you so far.

It's still a game. At the start of every contest, the umpire yells "Play ball!" He doesn't yell "Get to work!" Enjoy what you are doing. Far more is accomplished with an enthusiastic smile than with a disgruntled frown.

All sports unite people. Football is probably the most popular sport in America. Soccer is worldwide. I know of many golf fanatics that would give almost anything for a chance to play a round with Tiger Woods. Women's athletics are rapidly growing in popularity as are X-Games events. All sports teach us valuable lessons. They provide us with roles and role models. We learn the joy of competition, of camaraderie, of teamwork, of preparation, of success and of failure. All are lessons of the game. All are lessons for business. All are lessons for life.

WHAT KIND OF VOLCANO ARE YOU?

I'm not much of a science guy, but volcanoes fascinate me. It was a quirk of fortune that during one 13-month period, from April 1979 to May 1980, I had a first-hand experience with four active volcanoes. Three were in Italy and one was in the U.S. Two of these mountains were smoldering but calm. The other two were in various stages of eruption.

I went to Italy in 1979 as a crewmember of the USS Shenandoah, an old Navy repair ship that was on its final voyage. During an early stop in Naples, we were docked directly across the bay from Mount Vesuvius, a 4,000-foot active volcano. It is best known for erupting in 79 A.D. and burying the city of Pompeii. During my six week stay in Naples I had the chance to explore the mountain, and as mentioned in a previous essay, actually climbed to its summit. Several weeks later, our ship headed south to the island of Sicily. We were ported at Augusta Bay, in the shadows of Mount Etna. This volcano is much larger than Vesuvius and was showing distinct signs of impending geologic activity. Three days after leaving Augusta, Etna erupted. My third Italian volcano was Stromboli, which is an island mountain, rising from the floor of the Mediterranean Sea, north-west of Sicily. It is active and smoldering, and made for quite a sight as our ship passed a mile or two from its shores.

In May of 1980, no longer aboard the Shenandoah, I was asked to attend a Navy school in Bremerton, Washington. As fate would have it, we landed in Seattle's airport roughly six hours before Mount Saint Helens erupted. Bremerton is just a few hundred miles north of the volcano. The eruption of Saint Helen's was front page news, as it was perhaps the most violent geological event to ever occur on U.S. soil. I got to see four volcanoes in 400 days. No wonder I find them interesting.

At times people have been compared to volcanoes, usually in regards to anger and temperament issues. The phrase "to blow your top" and the term "venting" are both human attributes as well as volcanic references. A person who doesn't deal with anger very well by properly venting is more likely to erupt and blow his or her top. Everyone has a temper and everyone gets angry, but how we deal with that anger says a lot about the kind of person we are. It directly affects how we treat others, and how others will approach us. Everyone is a potential volcano. What kind are you?

Are you a Strato volcano? This type tends to sit dormant, appearing to be calm and unaffected by all that is going on around it. In reality, it is smoldering beneath the surface as both pressure and heat build toward dangerous levels. When it can no longer handle the intense pressure, a Strato will explode with sudden and violent force. Mount Saint Helens did this in 1980. People do it all the time. They put forth a calm exterior, internalizing stress and anger until they finally blow up. Their eruption takes friends, family and coworkers by surprise, since no one knew that there was anything wrong. These eruptions can be hurtful and cause great damage.

Are you a Shield volcano? As a rule, these are not great mountains, but cover a wide area. Many are found on the ocean floor as well as on various large islands, including Iceland. They tend not to explode but rather blanket the surface with a great many vents and hot spots. As you navigate your way across this terrain, you can never be quite sure when you will be vented upon. Shields are people who seem angry all of the time. They are constantly blowing off steam by criticizing people, places or things. It is a challenge to deal with such individuals, since there is no safe approach. As a result, Shields are often shunned and avoided by people who would rather not risk getting burned.

Are you a Cinder Cone? This volcano will grow rapidly, usually from a single geologic event. It has one vent, will blow off steam, and then recede into dormancy. You don't hear much about Cinder Cones because they are not very exciting. They simply get angry, let their displeasure be known, and then return to normal. There is nothing flashy or explosive about a Cinder Cone, and as a result, they do the least amount of harm.

So what kind of volcano are you? I think most of us would prefer to think of ourselves as Cinder Cones, but in truth we may at times be any of the three. Everyone gets angry and everyone has a need to express that anger, but when tempers flare, people get hurt. It is important to be aware of the situation from both sides. An environment where others can vent safely is beneficial to all. It is important to be able to express displeasures without hurting. To do so in a proper manner is something that requires tolerance, restraint, discipline and skill, but is ultimately worthwhile.

In most companies each year, a handful of talented and hardworking employees lose their jobs because their temper gets the best of them. Sometimes it is called "Hostile Work Environment." Other times it is insubordination. In worst-case situations, things get physical. It is always unfortunate and unnecessary. It is okay to get angry. It is okay to vent and express that anger. Just do it the right way. Don't be a Strato or a Shield. We need more Cinder Cones.

WHAT WAS I THINKING?

I have always considered myself to be a fairly open-minded person. I suspect most of us think of ourselves that way. No one wants to admit to holding racist or bigoted views. Just the same, we are naturally inclined to judge other people on some level, making assessments, both good and bad, based on a limited amount of information. Often our judgment is incorrect.

During a routine commute to work, I took notice of the car in front of me. It was a beat up old Mustang convertible with the top down. The driver was a small-framed individual who was wearing some sort of black hooded garment. At first look, it appeared to be a Muslim woman wearing a burqah or some other traditional Islamic garb. I found this to be rather peculiar since I would never equate an Islamic woman with a Mustang convertible. Then I saw that the driver was smoking a cigarette. I was now completely convinced that my eyes had deceived me.

A few blocks farther down the road, this driver yanked down the hood and revealed bright orange dyed hair which now flowed freely in the breeze. Definitely not a Muslim woman. As my perception changed, I thought that this person looked very much like the nice young woman who works at the coffee shop near my job. She is always friendly and quick with a smile. A bit eccentric maybe, but a very pleasant person. I smiled to myself, amused at how my first impression had been so inaccurate.

As my drive progressed, the road widened and I moved to the left of the Mustang, pulling alongside it at a traffic light. Curious, I turned my head right to see the driver. Again I had been completely wrong. It was not a woman in the car, but a young man, perhaps 20 years old or so. To go along with his long orange hair, this individual had a pierced eyebrow and numerous tattoos on his hands, lower arms and neck. I winced involuntarily when I first caught a glance of him. By the time I arrived at work a few moments later, I was questioning my eyesight, my judgment, and some aspects of my sanity. How could I have been so wrong on so many levels?

In a span of just over two miles, I had formed numerous incorrect opinions based on a very limited amount of information. Judgment was based on a person's car, clothes, hair color and several other characteristics. None of these things had much at all to do with the person.

Why wouldn't a Muslim woman be driving a late-model Mustang convertible? I know of nothing in their beliefs that would discourage them from owning such a car. It is probably no more peculiar than if a middle-aged, middle-class suburbanite like myself was behind the wheel. How would others have judged me? As for smoking, I have never seen a woman in a burqah smoking a cigarette, but I don't know enough about Islamic beliefs to assume that it doesn't happen.

During the stretch of time when I mistook the driver to be the girl from the coffee shop, my judgment was based on what I believed to be additional information. Since I thought I recognized this person, I was able to suspend prejudices, having already formed the opinion that this was a pleasant and likeable individual. Had this appeared to be someone else, I may have thought otherwise, thinking less of this person because of the cigarette and the orange hair.

When I finally saw exactly who was driving, I winced. This bothers me. I don't know this person. While I may dislike his style choices, I certainly do not have enough information to pass judgment. Perhaps he is a musician in a rock and roll band. Maybe he is an artist, or writes children's books. He could even be an undercover police detective who is wearing a disguise. Based on one look, I had already determined that he was a thug. This rush to judgment was completely unfair.

How do you judge people? Have you ever formed an opinion about someone based at least in part on their appearance, or age, or religious or political views? Most of us have. We all hold prejudices. This in itself does not make us a racist, a bigot, or a bad person, but it does cause us to draw incorrect conclusions about people. Our bias is often based on how we grew up, the people we currently surround ourselves with, and our past and present experiences in life. When we prejudge someone based on our prejudices and without the benefit of sufficient information, we do a great disservice to both the individual and ourselves.

WHY ANNIVERSARIES MATTER

1985 was a very important year for me because of three major events.

On May 19, I graduated with a Bachelor of Arts degree from the University of Connecticut. My degree was in Labor Relations. On May 20, I began working for the Walgreens Company, through which I am still employed. I was hired as an entry level manager for the starting pay of $6.90 an hour. While that would be considered below minimum wage by today's standards, at the time it was considered decent money for a starting position. Then, on August 10, 1985, I married Diane Jurgeilewicz in a small church service in Fairfield, Connecticut. Many years later, I am still making use of my degree, I still work for Walgreens, and Diane and I are still happily married. Nineteen-eighty-five was indeed quite a year.

Do anniversaries matter? So often as we get older, people refer to their birthday as "just another day." Aren't anniversaries just another day? To be honest, yes, they are. In the grand scheme of things, the university, the business world and Diane would have all done just fine without me. I would like to think that all have done better with than without, but no doubt all would have continued along their respective successful paths. Likewise, I would have found other courses to follow. With all of that in mind, why bother with anniversaries? I choose to celebrate them because I believe there is genuine value in recognizing milestones. Anniversaries are an opportunity to mark a point in time. It is then that we may reflect back and look forward.

Educational achievement is a milestone worth noting. That is why we celebrate graduations. The pursuit of academics is a difficult undertaking. Success in the classroom takes a substantial commitment of both time and effort. Has your high school or college education served you well? Is it time to consider returning to school, taking a class, or pursuing the next level of intellectual achievement? How about learning something simply because you want to? Is there a subject that you find interesting and want to know more about? Education for the sheer joy of learning is always a worthy endeavor. Recognizing important dates in one's education allows us a moment to reflect and ask these important questions.

Are you happy in your current job? Are you glad you chose this particular company as your employer? I must admit that after 10 years on the job I was not overly pleased with my situation and began to look elsewhere. I am glad I looked, but even more pleased that I chose to stay. Now after nearly 30 years I can look back and say that I did indeed choose well. We spend roughly a third of our lives at work, so fulfillment and job satisfaction are extremely important. Don't be afraid to ask yourself tough questions, and don't be afraid to look elsewhere. You may find something better, or as in my case, you may find that you are better off than you thought.

What about relationships? Are you in a relationship because it is fulfilling or simply because it is familiar? In any long term relationship there will be times when you or your partner grow bored or complacent, or feel neglected, or simply start to drift apart. Anniversaries are cause for celebration, but they are also cause for evaluation. Are you happy in your current situation? If your relationship is indeed all you ever hoped for, then seize the moment to reflect and rejoice. If not, then maybe you can use the event as a reason to fix things before they are broken beyond repair.

Other anniversaries, such as births, deaths and moments of personal accomplishment are also worth noting. Every year at the appropriate time, I recall and reflect on the death of my parents. I am grateful for the life they gave me and the lessons they taught. Likewise, on Veteran's Day, I celebrate the day I joined the U.S. Navy. My four years in the military in many ways helped to mold me into the person I am today. It is also my opportunity to give thanks to all fellow vets who have served our country.

Anniversaries are important. Regardless of your current situation, use these events to count your many blessings. I do. Despite all of life's ups and downs I can look back on the many years and know that in learning, earning and loving, I have been very, very fortunate. I hope you, too, can look back with the same pride, and forward with great optimism. Happy anniversary to all.

WHY EXPECTATIONS CAN LEAD TO MEDIOCRITY...OR GREATNESS

My daughter Emily played basketball for a small New England college. Since she did not have a car at her disposal during her freshman year, either my wife or I would occasionally make the one-hour drive up to the school and bring her home for the weekend. Often, these rides would result in some interesting and enlightening father-daughter conversations. In the course of one such talk, I asked her what the biggest difference was between her high school and college basketball teams. She quickly answered, "Expectations."

Emily went on to explain that her high school team wasn't very good, and everyone knew it. They were expected to win a couple of games, and then quietly disappear. Even after they posted victories in the first two games of the season against fairly difficult opponents, no one took notice. Collectively, the team began to realize that it didn't matter at all if they were expected to lose. What was important was that they expected to win. They may not have had the most talented team, but if they demanded excellence from themselves and played their hearts out for every minute of every game, good things would surely happen. Her team did not win the championship that year, but they did go on to have a very successful and winning season.

Her college team knew they were good, and so did almost everyone else. They were expected to win a lot of games and be a strong contender for the conference championship. But it takes more than just high expectations to win. After losing two of their first three games, her team quickly realized that just because they were good didn't mean it was going to be easy. They had to play their best and fully utilize their superior talent. Talent doesn't mean much if you don't come prepared to take on your opponent. Her team regrouped and swore that they wouldn't lose another game all season. While that didn't happen, they did go on to set a school record with 21 consecutive wins, finishing the season with a lofty 25-5 record.

How does this relate to corporate success? Every company has divisions, departments and individuals from whom not much is expected. The organization looks to get limited results because it wants to be realistic about circumstances, talent, and attainable goals. If you are one of those individuals, or work in a division or department where less is expected, it is not an acceptable practice to settle for your anticipated limitations. You have an obligation to demand and accomplish more. Likewise, every company has its high achievers. From them you expect greater results. If you fall into this category, should you be satisfied whenever you meet expectations? Absolutely not. Expectations should be a lower baseline, not an ultimate goal. Demand more. Achieve more.

In school we give a letter grade to judge how a student is doing. A student who meets expectations gets a C. The A and B grades are reserved for those who exceed that standard. Most companies have high standards. If you meet expectations, you are really doing quite well. But why stop there and settle for a C? With a little extra effort, an A+ might be well within your reach.

Expectations can be a recipe for mediocrity. It is good to know what the standards are, but only you know just how far you can go. It is only when you come prepared - and prepared to work hard - that greatness can be achieved. Never settle for the expectation of others. What are your own expectations? How high do you think you can reach? Your standards should always be higher than the ones that have been set for you by others. Don't let others tell you what you should be able to accomplish. Consider what is demanded, and then demand much more than that from yourself. Anything less would be settling for mediocrity.

WHY THEY ARE STILL THE BEST

From time to time, a few friends and I play a little game we call "Music Trivia Friday." Emailing from home, we exchange questions and comments pertaining to various aspects of pop culture. One topic that came up was a discussion as to what the best live concert we had ever seen was and why. For me the choice was easy. In 2002 I saw the Rolling Stones in Hartford, and in 1999 I saw Bruce Springsteen in Boston. Over the years I have probably seen 30 or 40 rock and roll shows. That's not a huge number but still it's a pretty good sampling. Naming the best two was easy. Anything else was a distant third.

Both shows were a feast for the senses. In each case, the artists performed for nearly three hours with a passion, energy, showmanship and musicianship that made them stand apart from the others. In the case of the Rolling Stones, I wasn't much of a fan before going to the show. I left as a committed devotee. With Springsteen, I was an avid fan with high expectations. His show easily surpassed anything I could have imagined.

Perhaps what impressed me most about these performers was the fact that they had been doing many of these songs for a very, very long time, and yet they still sounded fresh and new. At the time I saw them, Mick Jagger and Keith Richards had been doing "Satisfaction" for nearly 40 years. Likewise, Bruce and his E Street Band had been playing "Born to Run" for more than 25.

Thousands of shows. Good days and bad. It sounded new. I asked myself why. Surely by now they must be sick of playing the same chords and barking out the same lyrics over and over again. Surely it must become a dull routine. If it is, they certainly had me and 20,000 others fooled. As I thought about why they are so good, I also considered my own job and my many coworkers who have experienced some degree of longevity with one company. If these artists can stay at the top of their game after all these years, how can we do the same? Here are a few thoughts:

<u>They love what they do.</u> To watch Mick or Bruce play to an audience, or to see Keith Richards plugged into his guitar, you get the impression that there is no place on earth they would rather be at that moment. This is who they are and what they do. Anyone who has stayed at one company or one position for a significant span of time develops an

identity that is tied to the job. If you love what you do, then it is no great effort to continue performing to the best of your ability.

They enjoy being around their coworkers. Band-mates and coworkers come and go, but to work as a team it helps if you actually like and respect the people you work with. If you don't, it will show and the quality will suffer. Mick and Keith have had their differences, but when all is said and done they truly care for each other, their band-mates, and the many promoters, stagehands and roadies who keep them together.

They value and respect their audience. Before each show, Springsteen spends some time sitting in various seats throughout the arena to get a sense of what his concert will look and sound like to his audience. He works for them so it is important that they get the best possible quality and value for their dollars. Do you respect your customers? Are you doing everything you possibly can to give them the best product, service and value for their money?

They are constantly learning. Regardless of what your job is, it is constantly changing. New trends. New technologies. To remain at the top of your profession, you must be willing to learn and adapt. Likewise, you have to recognize when you have made a mistake, correct it if you can, then move on. Rock legends have to do this. So do you.

They reinvent the old. There are at least a dozen different arrangements for the song "Born to Run." By taking something that is old and reliable and reworking it, you can make it feel fresh and new. What ideas or important tasks are you currently doing that have become old, boring or routine? Is there something you can do to make them different, better, and more interesting?

Every day they do the best job they possibly can. This may sound trite but it is true. You aren't allowed to have an "off day." They happen but they shouldn't. Your customers, clients and coworkers are counting on you to be at your very best for every minute of every day. That may not be possible, but you have to try. You cannot let them down.

A lot of people have jobs that they stay at for many years. A lot of people have risen quickly through the ranks of a company to achieve a high degree of success within their chosen profession. What is rare is for someone to stay at the top of his or her game for a very long period of time. The Stones and Springsteen have done this. I did not start out as a Stones fan. They made me one. I had high expectations for the Springsteen show. He exceeded them. How many new customers or clients will you encounter today? How many of them will leave as fans of your company? How many of your long-time regulars will you interact with today? How many of them will be smiling as you once again remind them of why they choose to buy your goods and use your services?

WORD ON THE STREET IS...

I'm not a Barry Manilow fan. While I respect him as an accomplished entertainer, I have never been to one of his shows, nor do I intend to go anytime soon. That having been said, Barry Manilow is a marketing genius. He began writing popular jingles for television commercials in the late 1960's. Some of his more popular works are embedded in our Americana. *You deserve a break today... (McDonald's). Like a good neighbor State Farm is there. I am stuck on Band-Aid 'cause Band-Aid's stuck on me....*From there he went on to pop stardom, charting numerous hits and selling millions of albums.

A few years ago his popularity began to wane. The Las Vegas Hilton took a chance and hired him to do a series of shows. Manilow knew that this gig could make him or break him for several years to come. He spent several months preparing and honing his act into a two-hour extravaganza. That was good but not good enough. He needed a plan, a solid strategy that would tell the world that this easy-listening entertainer was back in a big way. The solution turned out to be quite simple. Manilow did a series of free shows for cab drivers and hotel workers. That was all it took. What began as a limited engagement turned into a two-year run. Whenever someone asked a cabby or bellhop what the best show in town was, Manilow's name came up. Word of mouth made Barry Manilow one of the hottest tickets in town.

One of the most popular pizzerias in the Northeast is Pepe's in New Haven, Connecticut. The place has been around since 1926 and has never sold anything other than pizza. You cannot get pasta, a sandwich, or soup. Just pizza and maybe a salad. It does one thing and does it very, very well. As a result, its need to advertise is minimal. For more than eighty years people would line up and wait for hours to eat there. Why? Word of mouth. Locals from the neighborhood would take friends and family there. The out-of-towners soon spread the word about the incredible pizza served at Pepe's. The place is so popular that when both Ronald Reagan and Bill Clinton were running for president, they chose Pepe's as a campaign stop. While for many years New Haven was its only location, they have recently opened several other restaurants throughout the state, as well as Yonkers, New York. Just as with the original location, people who leave these establishments cannot wait to tell others about the amazing food they got there. I have personally eaten at several of these restaurants, and will readily admit that it is worth the hype.

What makes word of mouth so valuable to Barry Manilow and Pepe's Pizza is not the buzz. The buzz would quickly die if they did not back it up nightly with great quality and a great show. Barry and Pepe's have to be at their very best every single night. If they start to sacrifice quality, it will immediately impact their business. There will still be plenty of word of mouth. The cabbies and locals will quickly turn on them and warn others to stay away. Unless they can continue to exceed expectations, night after night, they surely will fail.

So, what is the word of mouth at your company? Do you exceed expectations every day? Do people eagerly recommend you to other customers and clients? Or do they say, "I wouldn't bother with them. Their quality and service is lacking." If your company is to continue to have success, you, too, will have to be at your very best 24 hours a day, 365 days a year. Your patrons will not tolerate anything less.

YOU MAY NOT SUCCEED, BUT YOU DON'T HAVE TO FAIL

Did you ever try your absolute hardest at something only to fail miserably? You work tirelessly at it. You get help from others. You do everything you can possibly do to succeed, but don't. You feel frustrated, humiliated, angry and disappointed. You question your ability and your resolve. You are embarrassed because you let yourself and others down. You just want to run away and hide. Trust me, if you have ever had such an experience, you have plenty of company.

One of my favorite books is "*The Old Man and the Sea*," by Ernest Hemingway. It is the story of Santiago, a poor Cuban fisherman who has been struggling for weeks without much success. Tired and hungry, he continues to go to the sea in the hope that his fortunes will turn favorable. Finally, he hooks what seems to be the largest fish in the ocean, a giant and legendary blue marlin. Others have heard tales of this fish, but no one could catch it. Santiago fights the fish, the weather, and the sea for what seems like an eternity before the fish is finally conquered. Despite this great victory, success still does not come his way. He ties the giant fish alongside his small boat. As he makes his way back home, sharks tear at the body of the fish, leaving him with nothing more than a large skeleton. Santiago returns to the village in despair, but the villagers do not see him as a failure. He did, after all, conquer the legendary giant.

The book was an immediate best seller. Hemingway was often questioned about the possibility of deep and hidden meanings in the story. To this query he consistently replied that there was only one meaning intended. A person may be beaten but not destroyed. The absence of victory is not always defeat.

So often we hear inspiring catch phrases and clichés such as "Failure is not an option" and "Winning isn't everything. It's the only thing." They are nice words and great motivational lines, but they are not always realistic.

As embarrassing as it is for me to admit this, I was once fired from a job. About halfway through my senior year of college, I ran out of money. I interviewed for a position as a plant manager at a small factory that manufactured plastic bottles. Much to my surprise, I was hired. I was completely unqualified for the job. I knew nothing of how to run a factory. I simply knew how to interview well. The company was convinced it was getting a rising star. I was hoping I could learn on the job. It just didn't work out. I worked long hours, got help from everyone available and still did not succeed. They were unhappy with me, and I was completely miserable. After six months they let me go. It was a tremendous blow to my ego, but I survived. I returned to college, finished up my degree, and moved on to other, more successful endeavors. In many ways that failure led me to future victories.

All managers are routinely called upon to make difficult and unpleasant decisions. None is more painful than having to tell a good person, who is giving his or her best effort, that their best is not good enough. At times the blow can be lessened by offering the employee a different position where the chance of success is greater. When that is not the case, there is solace in the hope that the individual will learn from the experience and use it to move on to future accomplishments. Once the decision is made it is up to that person to decide if it is failure or just a setback.

Success is never guaranteed, but defeat does not always mean failure. It is a test of character. We all have setbacks and obstacles to overcome, both at work and elsewhere. Adversity can either drag you down or drive you forward. Learn from your stumbles and missteps. Don't let failing to succeed turn into succeeding to fail.

DON'T BE A JERK

A number of years ago I read a short business article entitled "Beware of Talented Jerks." Though less than a thousand words long, it was one of the most inspiring, motivating and thought-provoking pieces I have found on the subject. The premise is simple. In any given organization you will find a number of extremely intelligent, talented and hardworking individuals who deliver outstanding results, but are poison to anyone who comes in contact with them. They are complete jerks.

You know the type. They may make the numbers, but they do so at the expense of their coworkers. They are bullies, boors and tyrants. Almost no one wants to work with them, and even fewer would want to work for them. Often they harass and berate others while taking credit for the accomplishments of their peers. They don't respect others, withhold information rather than teach, and care more about their own career path than the success of the organization. These individuals often belittle coworkers, criticize incessantly, never praise the success of others, and manage through fear and intimidation.

The truth is, these people are more trouble than they are worth. Many companies will tolerate them because they bring results. This is shortsighted and clearly a mistake. The tactics of a few talented jerks will cause others to underachieve and ultimately leave, thereby dragging down the entire organization.

Everyone knows a talented jerk, but how do you know if you are one? Is it possible that in your drive for success, you are wearing blinders, oblivious to how your work, words and actions are affecting others? No one wants to acknowledge the possibility that his or her own deportment may be having a negative effect on coworkers, but it certainly does happen. Are you a talented jerk? Consider the following:

1. It is possible to treat people fairly and still not treat them well. Treating people fairly means that you follow the rules, show consistency and ensure that no one gets preferential treatment. Technically, you can treat everyone poorly, but if all receive the same harsh consideration, it may indeed be construed as fair. Talented jerks will hide behind rules and policies, without ever considering the value of a more flexible approach. Treating people well means that you take into account their needs and desires. Your actions are based on loyalty and mutual respect. An

employee who is treated fairly will generally show up to work and do a good job. An employee who is treated well is more inclined to go above and beyond without being asked. Such a person feels that he or she is part of a team where everyone looks out for everyone else.

2. There is a big difference between not lying, telling the truth, and being honest. Not lying allows you to omit information rather than falsify it. The truth is based upon cold, hard facts. Honesty requires some soul-searching, clear thinking, and the guts to speak up and tell others something that you know they do not want to hear. Honesty also means being able to tell someone whom you don't particularly like that they did a good job and are a valuable part of the team. Most people want you to tell them what they want to hear. I prefer to be told what I need to know. I am a big fan of the open door approach, but sometimes a private, closed-door conversation is even better. You can be honest with me and I will be honest with you. That's a big part of how we treat each other well.

3. It is possible to be a great scoundrel without actually doing anything wrong. This point is really important. Talented jerks are masters at this. There are athletes who will only play hard or show their humanitarian side when the cameras are on them. In business, some employees work their hardest when the boss is around and then slack off the minute he or she leaves. Some talented jerks will only help others when they think it will be noticed or benefit themselves in some manner. While there is nothing wrong with a little self-promotion, it is important to realize that you are part of a team. Your teammates are counting on you to be your best and do your best, even when the lights are not shining on you.

Are you a talented jerk? Don't think it isn't possible. All of us, myself included, have had moments when we've become arrogant, stubborn, cocky and headstrong. We all have the potential to be a bully. I believe you and I can limit such behavior to minimal isolated incidents. Ideally, we can treat each other with honesty, fairness, kindness and respect in almost any situation. Those who cannot are of little use to the organization, regardless of their ability.

SAY WHAT YOU MEAN. MEAN WHAT YOU SAY. BE MISUNDERSTOOD.

Back in 1979 I met a college English professor whom liked to tell the story of an award-winning poet that he knew. In the late 1950s, this particular writer published a poem entitled "Cancer Cells." The poem received national attention. It was all about the threat that the Soviet Union, and communism in general, posed to our way of life. It warned of the evils of Russian imperialism spreading like cancer through Asia and Europe, jeopardizing our security and destroying weak and less healthy democracies.

That is how the poem was interpreted. Unfortunately, the interpretation was completely wrong. The real story behind the story is that the writer was leafing through a copy of Life Magazine when he came across a photo essay that included a collection of pictures of cancer cells. It turns out that the poem "Cancer Cells" really was about cancer. The intellectual community refused to believe this. It argued that he must have at least been thinking about communism when he wrote it. Numerous heated debates followed. After a while, the writer became angry and disillusioned over being so blatantly misinterpreted. He stopped giving interviews and even gave up writing for a while.

In 1982, singer John Mellencamp had a number one hit with his song "Jack and Diane." The song is about two teenagers from the Midwest who are struggling with the transition from adolescence to adulthood. To this day, people will stop Mellencamp and ask him who the "real" Jack and Diane are. Are they still together? What are they doing these days? The truth is that these two characters don't exist. They never did. Mellencamp would try to explain that it's just a song and that Jack and Diane are simply two people whom he made up and put to music.

As in the case of the poet, the public usually isn't satisfied with that answer. Eventually, Mellencamp gave up on telling the true story and began explaining that Jack and Diane are a combination of several people that he knew while growing up in Indiana. This response seems to satisfy most people. Unlike the poet, the songwriter doesn't get angry or upset about being misunderstood. He thinks it's rather exciting. He believes a song only belongs to him until it goes out to the public. Once a song is published, it belongs to the audience. If the audience thinks Jack and Diane are real people, then it means he succeeded in making a strong connection with something that his audience can relate to. To make that connection is probably the most important and satisfying thing that any writer, musician or artist can do.

Over the years I have written a number of editorial pieces that have garnered some intense and impassioned responses. Some were positive, some were negative. When you identify a certain personality type or characteristic and then publicly praise or condemn it, people tend to take notice. If I have written my piece well, both my criticism and praise will remind readers of someone they know. If the piece is really well written, they may even suspect that they were the subject. Was I thinking of them when I wrote the article? Doubtful, but I am thrilled if they feel that way.

Like Jack and Diane, my personal references are usually a composite of several people I have known. Some are co-workers, past and present. Some are relatives. For the most part, I am just trying to offer some good information that is worth thinking about. Like Mellencamp my goal is to make a connection and elicit a response. That response, even if it is a negative one, is a powerful form of praise. I assure you, the audience, that whatever your interpretation may be - of a song, a poem, essay or painting - if it resonates with you and if it makes you think or feel something, then the meaning you assign to it will be absolutely correct, and the author, no matter how misunderstood, will have done his or her job well.

About the Author

Ralph Yourie is a manager, writer, and U.S. Navy veteran. In 1985 he graduated from the University of Connecticut, with a degree in Labor Relations. Born and raised in New Jersey, he now lives in Ellington, Connecticut with his wife Diane, daughters Emily and Allison, two cats, and a rescue greyhound named Camille. His beagle, Truman, who is the topic of one of the stories in this book, has gone to dog heaven.

The cover design and illustration for this book was done by the author's daughter, Allison Yourie.

CPSIA information can be obtained at www.ICGtesting.com
Printed in the USA
BVOW02s1843120415

395729BV00001B/3/P

9 781770 972803